BRINGING MOM HOME

HOW TWO SISTERS MOVED THEIR MOTHER OUT OF ASSISTED LIVING TO CARE FOR HER UNDER ONE AMAZINGLY LARGE ROOF

SUSAN SOESBE

REND
PRESS

REND
PRESS

CONTENTS

To caregivers all over the globe: God sees.

PREFACE

This is the story of what happened when I tried to do the right thing without knowing how it would all work out. When it was all over, the result was surprising enough that I thought you should be able to read about it. So I wrote it, with some help and a lot of editing.

All of this really happened. I based this book on blogposts I wrote and on notes, texts, and emails my sister and I made on the journey. Mostly, though, it's based on my memory, checked against the memories of others. To the best of my knowledge, everything here is true, unvarnished, unembellished and free of GMOs and pesticide residues. Some pseudonyms are used to protect privacy.

NEW JERSEY TO CALIFORNIA

JANUARY 2014

*M*aybe it was just a big fat coincidence, but when I got the call my suitcase was already packed, and everything else --from futon to salad spinner-- was locked in large metal moving containers. So the next day, just like that, I walked away from my life in New Jersey and shuffled through security in a sea of grim-faced travelers in dark coats and salt-stained boots. The containers still sat on the curb in front of my apartment in West Orange. What used to be my apartment.

Of course I got the middle seat, between two women. One clutched a novel. The other listened to something through earbuds, her eyes closed. They glanced up when I pointed to my seat and silently made room for me.

When we reached cruising altitude, I could finally do what I'd waited to do for forty-eight hours. I leaned forward, head in hands, tensed to remain strictly within the rectangular prism of personal space allotted by the airline, and wept in noiseless convulsions. I sucked the stale air into my lungs and meted it out slowly, gulped and blew my nose in strict silence, and when it seemed to be winding down, I found myself fighting another sob, as if painfully disgorging a dry pellet. I cried for Mom, lying unconscious in a hospital bed, and for my sister and her husband, who gave up their perfect little house, probably for nothing. I cried for my lost idyllic road trip with the kids. It seemed I'd gotten everything horribly wrong, relinquished my good apartment and upset my whole life. I cried for Granny, dead these 27 years, and for poor old Aunt Lou, endlessly, mindlessly stringing beads. And while I was at it, I cried about the divorce. I realized suddenly there were a number of things all lined up and waiting to be wept over. Well, there was no time like the present, and there was nothing else to do. My grand plan was to drive to California, not fly, so I hadn't packed a book. My seat mates seemed oblivious. In a fit of subconscious foresight, I had brought a fistful of tissues. At least that part went as planned.

THE INCIDENT OF THE STOLEN CAR

My sister Claire and I didn't know when Mom crossed the line from living to dying. At first we thought she was just eccentric. Hadn't she always been different from other moms?

After Dad died in 2002, Mom moved from California to Texas, to be near her sisters, Bobbie and Lou. Claire and I flew out to visit her from time to time over the next ten years. Then we began to notice she was sort of *off*. We'd compare notes after each visit, Claire in California and I in New Jersey. Sure, people change as they get older, but how could we know what was normal at age seventy-nine?

During one of these visits, I was lying on the guest bed, which was basically my old twin bed with elderly blankets and pillows on it, when Mom knocked on the door.

"Susan," she exclaimed. "My car's been stolen."

I jumped up. "What? What makes you think that?"

"It's not out in the driveway."

I heaved myself out of bed and hurried to the front window. There was no SUV in the driveway, just some ragged brown streaks where pecan pods had stained the white cement. On a hunch, I strode to the garage, Mom following as fast as she could, which wasn't fast at all. I yanked open the door, revealing the Explorer. "Here it is," I said, flourishing my hand like Carol Merrill on *Let's Make a Deal.*

She spluttered "How did that get there?"

Later, this episode would stand out in my memory as The Moment I Realized Ginny Was Not Quite Right.

CHECKING MOM'S DRIVER'S LICENSE

MARCH 2012

*N*ow that we suspected Mom was not quite right, Claire and I began to stagger our visits, each of us flying out to Texas twice a year for a week. We'd noticed changes. For one thing, Mom rarely drove anymore. She said she couldn't find her way home.

In March of 2012, it was my turn to visit Mom, this time with my daughter. In the cab from the airport, Deborah texted her friends while I leaned back and let acres of scrub oak hurry past, punctuated by an occasional filling station or strip mall. *It's so big out here,* I thought. *We're not in New Jersey anymore, Toto.* Fields of crimson and yellow Indian paintbrush, and blue bonnets bright as sapphires, rushed past in a blur. Mom loved the wild flowers and trees, but she'd always wanted to live in a sturdy house which kept the plants and animals outside where they belonged. So when she moved, she chose a new housing development in Temple, where the recently-laid asphalt streets were lined with substantial brick houses, lawns like putting greens, backyards protected by stockade fences. The pavement was so smooth it seemed weirdly Stepford-like. You'd never see streets like these in New Jersey.

I liked Mom's house. It felt light and large, with soaring ceilings and plenty of windows. A mature Southern live oak, selectively spared in the recent construction, spread its branches over the lush front yard like Christ the Redeemer gazing down on Rio de Janeiro.

The morning after our arrival, as the three of us were sitting at the beat-up folding table in the kitchen, I steered the conversation toward the subject of photos. I pulled out my wallet and remarked, "Look at the terrible photo on my driver's license." I showed Mom the photo, which revealed two startled-looking eyes like Toll House morsels poked hastily into Pillsbury biscuit dough, and mouse-colored hair in two tentative lumps on either side of my head. Deborah brought forth her license, which wasn't terrible at all. It's hard to take a bad photo of a pretty young woman with big blue eyes and Disney-princess hair. I appeared to have been roughly summoned to a secret tribunal in the middle of the night, but Deborah looked like an advertisement for styling products. "Hey," she said, examining my license with uncharacteristic interest, "yours expires this year."

I turned to my mother and asked, conversationally, "When does yours expire?"

She asked me to fetch her purse from her room, where

it always sat next to the bed like a dutiful but weary pug. Extracting her license, she remarked disgustedly, "I don't know what it is about the DMV, but they always make my hair look even worse than usual."

For years, Mom had waged war with her hair, struggling with curlers and combs and styling products to make it conform to a mysterious and unreachable ideal. I said, "Let me see." There was the familiar fake smile, the one she used for sales clerks and government employees. Her watery blue eyes peered through bifocals, and she wore a loose tee shirt whose primary appeal was, I was sure, its comfort. And no makeup, as usual. She gave that up when I was still a child. Too expensive, and too much trouble. Her hair always looked the same to me: short, faded, tightly permed, utterly indifferent.

That night on the phone I reported to Claire that Mom's license was not due to expire for several years. Unfortunately.

CHECKING MOM'S FINANCIALS

While I was gathering intelligence, Claire emailed my next assignment: take Mom to Jackson-Hewitt to assure the people there that we were keeping an eye on her finances. Apparently, they were beginning to feel uncomfortable about filing tax returns for her.

As I read Claire's message, I imagined her in her living room, perched rigidly upright on a brown leather couch, a sliver of pillow tucked into the small of her back, tap-tap-tapping at the laptop balanced on her updrawn knees. It was after noon in California, and the sun would be winking lazily through the big front windows. She would most likely be eating freshly-baked chocolate chip cookies and drinking heavily-creamed decaf.

The tax professionals had good reason to feel uncomfortable. Five years ago, Mom got into a bind and called Claire for help. A man from Speedwell Financial had come to her house and sold her a questionable financial instrument for $20,000. Shortly afterward, when she became uneasy and backed out of the transaction, she was refunded only $11,000.

Claire asked, "Mom, what happened?"

"That man had a silver tongue," said Mom. "He talked me into things I didn't understand."

Claire was livid, but she couldn't recover the $9,000. Mom was deeply ashamed. She said, "I didn't want you to know how stupid I was."

Claire set Mom up with a Certified Financial Planner, and carefully crafted a script for her to read if anyone from Speedwell called again: "I am working with a different advisor now. I will not be buying any more of your products. Please do not contact me again." This was polite enough to be Texan, yet firm enough to do the job. If she remembered to use it. "Don't you worry," Mom drawled, shaking her head. "From here on out, I'll be the biggest naysayer you've ever seen."

Three years later, someone from Speedwell called Mom again, claiming, "It's time for your review." Mom didn't remember the script, but she smelled a rat, and emailed Claire, who contacted Speedwell directly and told them them in no uncertain terms that they were to leave Mom alone. Claire's anger, as she recounted this story for me, was palpable.

Recalling this incident, I felt a wave of compassion. Mom had always had a weakness for charming young men, but she hadn't always been this vulnerable, and she knew it.

TAKING MOM TO WALMART

oday, we were off to Walmart. As I pulled into a parking spot, a large African-American woman exited the store. "Just look at that big old fat black woman," breathed my mother, as if remarking on a scandal. "How can she stand to be like that?"

I wondered if she were referring to the woman's size or her blackness, but decided not to request clarification on this point. "Now don't get out till I can come around and help you," I said.

I leaped out of the car and ran around to the passenger's side before she could disobey me, and extracted her from the high seat. She was as light as a child, a bundle of brittle bones in a stained white tee and blue polyester pull-ons. She could certainly afford new clothes, but how could I convince her to buy them? She reflexively resisted spending money on anything. I was still marveling that she had insisted on reimbursing me for the cab fare when we arrived, which had been no small sum.

Mom used to be about five and a half feet tall, but seemed much shorter now, bent over like that. Her hands were all tendons and ropy veins, covered loosely with skin and dotted with liver spots.

She grabbed a stray shopping cart to lean on, like a walker. Five years ago, she had a hip replaced, but never followed up with physical therapy. This omission, combined with untreated scoliosis and osteoarthritis, led her to avoid ambulation whenever it was not strictly required. I took my place by her side as she made her cramped way to the entrance, hunched, forearms on the handle. Her steps were short and shuffling, and the sun was hot on my forehead. Somehow, the sun is hotter in Texas, hotter even than it is in California. It comes straight up to your face like a puppy. I asked, "Why don't you get a real walker, Mom?"

"I just don't want to give in to that."

Ten years ago, when Dad was overrun with cancer and only weeks from death, she used phrases like, "if your dad gets better." If she didn't give in to something, it wouldn't happen.

I sighed and thanked God for air conditioning, which was only steps away, and which I knew Walmart would provide generously.

GETTING MOM TO WEAR
THE NECKLACE

*B*ack at the house, I unloaded my purchases. Now there was real food for Deborah and me: alfalfa sprouts, avocados, tomatoes, broccoli. Deborah piled fresh cucumber slices and grape tomatoes into a Corelle bowl and retreated to the computer room. But each item I extracted from the grocery bags was a source of horrified fascination for Mom, whose mental list of approved foods was narrow and tended toward boxed and canned varieties. While I prepared lunch, she sat with her elbows on the folding table, chin on hands, and remarked, "what *is* that nasty stuff?"

"Chicken breast, avocado and alfalfa sprouts on whole wheat," I said.

She grimaced. I leaned on the counter, savoring my sandwich and refusing to be drawn in. She almost looked disappointed. She said she wasn't hungry, but I quietly made her a half BLT, of which she ate half. I knew when she went to her room for a nap later she would dig into a secret cache of chocolates. And I would wash and dry the dull knife I used to hack apart the tomato, and the aqua melamine plates, and the mug that reads, "Maw, Come Git Yer Cawfee," all relics from my childhood. She never bought new kitchen tools or a proper kitchen set, just kept using the same battered folding chairs and plastic-topped table.

It was time to talk turkey. I pulled up one of the rickety chairs and sat down in front of her.

"Mom," I began, "I'm concerned about your living alone. The way you walk makes me nervous. I'm afraid you're going to fall and break a hip, and there wouldn't be anyone to help you."

"What makes you think I'd break a hip?" she said, as if this were an outlandish idea, as if it hadn't already happened once before.

"That's what you always read about. Old ladies living alone fall and break their hip. They get pneumonia, and that's the beginning of the end."

"Well, that's not going to happen to me," she smiled, patting my knee as if I were a child.

"How do you know?"

"Well, for one thing, I don't get up on chairs or stools or anything. And for another, Bobbie and I call *and* email every day to check up on each other."

There was that. Aunt Bobbie also drove over once a

week. They used to take turns driving to each other's houses, till Mom started getting lost. Nonetheless, if anything happened, it would take hours for Bobbie to figure it out, and even longer for her to drive over and check. "Didn't you get one of those Life Alert necklaces once?" I asked.

No, but she did have a pendant from ADT which could be used in an emergency. When I explained this and asked her to wear it like a necklace, she looked pained.

"I don't like to wear things around my neck. They get caught on my skin tags."

"Okay, how about you pin it onto your shirt? Keep the pendant with your clothes, and every morning when you get dressed, pin it somewhere you can reach it. If you fall, all you have to do is push the button, and pretty soon the police will come. It would make me and Claire feel a lot easier."

"Well, all right," she grumbled.

Later, Aunt Bobbie practically laughed in my face. "Ginny will never wear that thing, you can be sure about that," she asserted. What else could we do? Implant a chip?

Aunt Bobbie knew my mother better than anyone. She was only two years younger than Mom, but she stood up straighter and laughed more often. Her clothes were new and brightly colored. Her iron-gray hair was rolled into a compact bun at the nape of her neck, like a fat little chipmunk. She inherited my grandfather's wide cheekbones and cleft chin, but, thank God, Granny's sense of humor. Like Mom, she wore no makeup, but her weather-browned skin and wide smile made this omission less obvious. Unlike my mother, Bobbie enjoyed being outdoors, tending plants and observing wild things. Out there, she said, it's simple, and no one bothers you.

EMPOWERING MOM, IN THEORY

APRIL 2012

The following day I girded up the loins of my mind and resolved to clean Mom's bathroom. Ginny was never an assiduous housekeeper. Still, in better days she would never have let her toilet get this feculent. The tank was thick with dust. Even the books piled on it had a visible coating of powdery material. The bowl was strongly redolent of urine. Mom hobbled into the bathroom and hovered over me as I grimly bent to my task. "You don't have to do that," she protested. "You came here to visit, not to clean."

I leaned back on my heels and sighed. "Well, somebody has to do it. If it's not you, it'll be me or Claire. Unless," I looked at her squarely, "you hire someone to do it." There, I had thrown down the gauntlet.

Ginny had never paid anyone to clean her house. But I

could tell she was thinking, as I turned back to the bowl and scrubbed away.

LATER, at the computer, I pulled up the Merry Maids site to show her how easy it would be to hire a housecleaner. We stopped short of filling in the "want more info" request. She wasn't ready to pick up the gauntlet just yet.

While we were there, I showed her how she could have her favorite granola bars sent directly to the house. The computer was a portal, I explained. With her computer, my mother could call for help, order up housecleaners and granola bars. She could lean back in the captain's chair like Captain Picard, wave her hand and say, "Make it so." The world was hers to command . . . if she could remember how to do it.

TEXAS TO NEW JERSEY

*M*ission accomplished, for now. Deborah and I flew back to New Jersey where my youngest son Michael had been staying with Paul and Connie. Through the divorce and the loss of our house, the Oberlanders had been his safe harbor. Though they reconfigured their furniture, it seemed, almost daily, as if they lived in a dollhouse, they were delightfully consistent: she, tiny and animated, a whirlwind in a splashy tee shirt and jeweled sandals, he, a towering bald man who retrofitted his wife's speeches with parenthetical amendments. While I was at Mom's they drove Michael and their Nathan to choir practice and church in their overstuffed van, which was littered with Wendy's cups, sporting equipment, and spelling books. There were always high-calorie smells coming from the Oberlanders' tiny kitchen, and when Paul emerged bearing food, as he frequently did, it was shared around with glee. Michael would have been sleeping on one end of the lumpy L-shaped couch in the living room, Nathan and the dogs on the other end. I knew they would have been up half the night talking about girls, theology, sports, movies. Paul and Connie's front door was never locked, so when Deborah and I walked in unannounced, the dogs barked their heads off. Connie exclaimed delightedly, and Michael jumped up from the couch and engulfed us both in a lengthy, rocking hug, the kind that makes you laugh because you know you look silly but also because you don't care that you look silly. We chattered all the way back to our West Orange apartment.

In the pile of accumulated snail mail I found a pamphlet sent by a friend, entitled *Making Your Senior Housing Decision*. I sent it along to Claire to show to Mom on her next visit. In spite of our misgivings, my sister and I couldn't just move Mom like a chess piece. The rule in our family was *mind your own business*. Mom had to choose for herself. On the other hand, if the problem was that she was getting more and more confused, how could she decide to do something about it?

WE BEGIN PRAYING FOR A PRECIPITATING EVENT

MAY 2012

*T*he week after my return to New Jersey, Aunt Bobbie emailed Claire and me:

Ginny indicated Wednesday that she will soon make a big decision about whether or not she will move. I know Ginny likes the status quo, but her memory is getting really bad. I told her that the day she goes to Walmart and can't remember how to get home, that's the day it will become crucial for her to do something.

Meanwhile, Mom wrote:

```
I tried to go see the doctor on Tuesday,
but couldn't remember how to get there.
```

When I shared this email with Claire, she observed rather darkly:

I wonder if forgetting how to get to the doctor is on a par with not remembering how to get home from Walmart.

As I prayed about this, I got an idea. I began asking God for a Precipitating Event. I wanted something to happen that was scary enough to convince Mom she needed to move closer to one of us, but not so bad that she or anyone else was really hurt.

When I told Claire, she began asking God for this too.

IS THIS NORMAL?

JULY 2012

*I*n May, Mom emailed in size eighteen font:

My e-mail address has changed too soesf@yahoo.com. Please send me Benjamin's e-mail address. I lost all my addresses, too.

I sat at my computer, arms crossed, staring uneasily at the screen. Ginny was always the one to correct grammar and spelling offenses, defending the English language like the Pontifical Swiss Guard. And she used to write several pages at a time. How had I not noticed the phenomenon of the shrinking emails?

I was analyzing my mother's life now like a forensic detective, weighing and comparing, wondering whether the changes I saw were variations of normal, or evidence of disease. Then I remembered the scramble of papers on her computer desk back in Texas. She used to keep her papers stacked and filed and clipped together. Now there were torn-off scraps, Post-it notes, hairpins, pens and unsharpened pencils strewn about. I sighed and began typing out my older son Benjamin's address, and made a mental note to simplify her computer experience on my next trip to Texas.

THE PRECIPITATING EVENT

JULY 2012

*I*n July, my mother backed her car into a pickup at the Bush's Chicken drive-through. She couldn't remember if she had insurance, and neither she nor the truck's driver called the police. Later, when he appeared at her door with a repair estimate, she handed him a check for over $800. Somehow, Bobbie convinced Mom to tell Claire, and Claire told me. When I called Mom, she sounded tired. She said she was ready to move to California and "live in an old folks' home."

"You can come and live in New Jersey," I offered.

"Hahaha," she said drily. "You will *never* get me to live in *New Jersey.*" As if I were the spider and she the fly. She was sure New Jersey was full of potholes, mobsters, and brassy Italian women in shiny black pants, cooking meatballs and guzzling chianti. Also snow. She hated to be cold. No, back to sunny California she would go.

As I hung up the phone, I thought, *Well, in theory she'll go back to California.* She was able to voice her preference for California over New Jersey, but did she have what it took to get there? Or was it enough for her simply to allow Claire and me to move her? What if she changed her mind?

ESCAPE

SUMMER 1948

*I*n Ballinger, Texas, Ginny and Bobbie have been given a handful of coins and permission to go to the double feature in town. Somehow, their mother found the money, yet again, for her two young teens to spend a glorious Saturday afternoon in Hollywood. *A Song to Remember* and *Anchors Aweigh* are playing at The Palace. The girls are shy, but not too shy to pay the man at the glass booth twelve cents apiece for their tickets. They hasten past the concession stand. There's no money for Cokes or popcorn, but they are content to disappear into the cool darkness, find seats in the very center, and stare for hours at the immense screen.

Ginny and Bobbie settle in as the opening credits to *Anchors Aweigh* unroll. Frank Sinatra is too skinny, but that Gene Kelly is some dancer. Neither girl thinks much of Kathryn Grayson, but the music is lively and the plot is thin, just the way they like it. *A Song to Remember* is too hard to understand. Why is the girl named George, and why is she wearing men's clothes, when she should be wearing a beautiful dress? What a waste! The posters in front of the theater boast that this is "the screen's greatest romance," but clearly the film's promoters have forgotten Scarlett and Rhett's torrid relationship.

FOUR HOURS LATER, Ginny and Bobbie are standing on the curb outside The Palace, waiting for Daddy to pick them up in the faded Chevrolet. Mama wants them home before dark. Home is two rooms on the outskirts of town with an outhouse and a brief slanted porch on which the girls sometimes play with paper dolls. Later, in the bed they share, the sisters dream of Gene Kelly, of satin dresses and feather boas, gleaming pianos and candelabras. Maybe tomorrow after church they can escape again.

CLAIRE VISITS MOM

Shortly after the Precipitating Event, my sister and her son Joel visited Mom. Claire called me that night, quite discomposed.

"When we got here, she was surprised to see us. I told her we had discussed this and she had written it on her calendar. And, Sues, she was *astonished* to see 'Claire and Joel' on her calendar, where she'd written it just a few weeks ago."

Mom then sank into a chair, my sister told me, head down and elbows on knees, silent and trembling. Claire said, "I really thought she might be having a stroke. I kept asking her, 'What's wrong? Are you okay?' And she said 'I just don't understand why this is happening to me.'"

Poor Claire. Poor Mom.

"I felt so sorry for her," said my sister, lowering her voice, though Mom's room was all the way on the other side of the house. "But I didn't cry in front of her. I distracted her by challenging her to a game of Rummikub."

"Isn't it strange," I interjected, "that she can't remember that you and Joel were coming for a visit, but she can still play a complex game like Rummikub?"

"Oh, it's not all that hard, and she's been playing it for years with Bobbie every week. But wait till I tell you what I found in her room."

"What?" I breathed.

"When I went in there, I was hit with a *very* strong odor of urine. There was a potty by the bed, one of those portable ones. And it had about an *inch* of dark yellow liquid." I could hear the outrage in her voice.

"So? People get old, they have to pee in the middle of the night, they can't get to the bathroom in time, so they get a potty. What's upsetting about that?"

"Sues, she never empties it. How can you pee in the potty night after night and just *leave* it like that? How can she stand the smell? Doesn't she care?"

"Maybe she's afraid she'll spill it."

"I don't know," Claire responded wearily. "You can bet I cleaned that thing within an inch of its life. I didn't say anything to her about it, though. I knew she would just get defensive, and I was too upset about the whole thing. I'm only telling you because I need to tell someone."

Poor Mom, I sighed to myself. Her personality was still there but her memory and reason were eroding. Maybe she'd been brave all along, and we hadn't noticed it. The worst of it was, she knew just enough to know she didn't know enough.

As we talked, I could see Claire stretched out on my old bed with its antiquated pillows and blankets. I guessed she'd had a good cry, alone in the guest room, before calling me.

Poor Claire. Her adolescence was stormier than mine, with more tears and door-slamming. But no shouting. We didn't shout. She should have been the one to move 3,000 miles away instead of me. But she stayed, and married Arthur, and they lived close enough to Mom and Dad to visit regularly. As the older daughter, she always felt more responsibility for our parents, and more upset with them when she disagreed with their choices. So I couldn't tell her, there on the phone, "You take things too hard," especially since I didn't know if this was true. So I said, "I'm really glad you and Joel are there with Mom, and you did a great job with the potty *and* not saying anything to her about it."

I'd known for some time there were things about Mom that upset my sister. I always thought she was overreacting, like she did when she was fifteen. But how could I know what was worth getting worked up about? She had always lived closer to Mom, visited regularly, and therefore had many more chances to get annoyed. I decided to begin praying for Claire's heart. Whether her perspective was right or not, her distress was real. And I loved her.

When do distress, disgust and anger turn into grief? Claire said goodnight and we hung up, and I knew she would lie in the dark and grieve.

MOM DECIDES, SORT OF

*T*he next morning, she got Mom to read *Making Your Senior Housing Decision,* and they looked at assisted living websites together. Mom wanted to know how much it would cost.

This time Claire was the boots on the ground, and I was the cool strategist, helping her plot the next move. As she made her daily reports, I lay on the thick carpeting in my West Orange apartment with the phone pressed to my ear, eyes closed, and imagined the goings-on at Mom's house. I could see them in the computer room, Claire sitting carefully upright in a flimsy folding chair, one hand on the mouse and the other resting lightly on Mom's shoulder. Mom would be hunched in the padded office chair, her bent spine permanently listing left, and leaning forward to peer at the screen with her one good eye. Joel, tall and willowy in classic nerd glasses, would be summoned from time to time to help with computer problems, but he was more likely to be sleeping, eating or listening to music. A few years ago, when he and Michael were visiting her at the same time, Mom bought them matching Razor scooters. They'd been all over the neighborhood then enjoying their preteen freedom, carefree cousins sucking on popsicles and racing on the smooth black asphalt. Funny, I'd forgotten that.

Claire and Mom began their Internet search near the home on Prospect Place where Claire and her husband Arthur lived. They found a promising facility called Omnia. Mom asked, "If I move, what would I do with all my stuff?"

"Take whatever you want with you, and we'll take care of the rest."

Claire thought she, Arthur and I could team up to take Mom and her favorite things to California in a moving van. One of us could dispose of the remaining items. She expected Arthur would have a window of time in his off-season.

"Well," I told my sister, "If we can think of something to do with Michael for the month of August, and if Arthur's available to drive Mom to California, I can be the sorter. Can we get Mom into Omnia that quickly?"

Claire would find out.

LOVE WITHOUT MEMORY

Meanwhile, she invited our cousins, Uncle John's girls Pam and Kim for a visit. The topic of conversation was, of course, our grandmother. We called her Granny, but Mom and her siblings called her Mama. By any name she was a stitch. Claire and Mom and the cousins gathered in the living room and drank sweet tea, trading stories about Granny: the time she suddenly yanked off her pants in a panic because there was a single, inexplicable fire ant in her underwear; that she kept dress-up clothes in a box for us all, even the adults, to dress up and clown around; how she called her cat "Snow Billiard." Granny was gone now, but she was still making them laugh. And then Claire realized Mom was crying. Not because her mother was dead, but because she couldn't remember any of these things, couldn't remember Mama at all.

Claire suddenly recalled that when Dad died nine years ago Mom couldn't remember enough about his life to write his obituary. At the time, she told herself it was because Mom was in shock.

THE NEUROLOGIST SPEAKS
JULY/AUGUST 2012

That night on the phone, my sister and I were forced to acknowledge yawning gaps in our mother's memory. She didn't remember where either of us was born. Four Christmases ago, Michael, Deborah and I drove her from Texas to Tennessee --a two-day journey-- but she could not recall a single thing about that trip. Even photographs couldn't jog her memory. She didn't argue with us, just shook her head and said, "I see that's me in the picture, and I know y'all aren't lying. But I don't remember a thing about it."

And she'd lost so much weight. While taking out the trash last year, a strong wind caught the bin she was pulling and blew her over.

When Claire first told me that Mom had been blown over, I laughed like a madman and then felt horribly guilty. Still, I hoped she would take it as motivation to eat more.

But I saw now it wasn't that she *wouldn't* take care of herself. She *couldn't* take care of herself.

A visit to the neurologist that week confirmed my assessment. He told Claire Mom had vascular dementia. He was very concerned about her "mild cognitive impairment."

This was mild?

The good doctor had seen a case or two of dementia before. He knew we needed him on our side. He gently described assisted living to Mom, and advised her to move to a facility in California. Mom had always taken the word of a doctor as gospel truth. Perched on the edge of the chair in the examining room, she attended carefully to the exalted man in the white lab coat. Claire was both relieved and worried: relieved to have professional endorsement, but worried that Mom wouldn't even remember this conversation when they left the office.

Claire wasted no time putting her name on Mom's accounts and paying her bills. In Mom's eyes, the doctor's edict carried the weight of a papal bull. She was, if not happy, at least cooperative.

MY SISTER'S HEART

AUGUST 2012

*D*eborah made arrangements to stay with Michael while I was in Texas for the Big Move. The two of them began planning a relaxing, Mom-free time. As far as I was concerned, all they'd have to do was keep themselves alive and bring in the mail.

And Claire's heart was softening. She called me one morning on her daily walk to report in.

"Well," she began. "God is helping me deal with Mom in a more understanding way."

I stretched out on the carpet and tucked a throw pillow behind my head. "I'm all ears."

She laughed. "Well, yesterday I was fiddling around in the kitchen, trying to decide what to have for lunch. I've basically given up asking her 'What would you like for breakfast or lunch or whatever?' because she invariably says she's not hungry."

"Yeah. She's never hungry. I don't get that. You'd think she'd be hungry at least *some* of the time," I put in.

"Right. But this time I decided to see if *she* would bring up the subject of eating. I'd boiled an egg earlier that day, and she asked me, 'What are you going to do with this egg?' I told her I was thinking about making egg salad with it, and would she like some egg salad if I put pickle and onion in it?"

"What did she say?"

I could hear the smile in my sister's voice. "She said yes, and I thought she meant to put it in the fridge for later. But I wanted to do all I could to tempt her to actually *eat* the stuff, so I asked her how much pickle to put in, and how much onion, et cetera. She watched me carry out each step, and stir it all up with mayo. And then she ate the whole thing for lunch!"

"Wow. The whole thing?" I was incredulous. Mom ate as much as an average two-year-old, so that was truly impressive.

"Yup."

I could imagine Claire's cooking show featuring the antiquated tools in Mom's kitchen, those dull knives and seventies-era saucepans. I fleetingly wondered what it would be like to have only an obsolete stock of mental tools at one's disposal, and no hope for a replacement set.

Claire added, "I think God is helping me see her in a more compassionate way."

"Awesome," I said, giving the Almighty a silent two-thumbs-up salute.

"Yeah. I discovered she hasn't balanced her checking account in almost a year-"

"What?" I interjected. "Are you kidding? Our mom?"

"-so I explained to her, very evenly and low-key as possible, that I was going to have to do what the doctor recommended, which was to handle her finances for her. I expected some resistance, but she just made some remarks to the effect that 'it sucks to get old.'"

I was still reeling over that delinquent checkbook. But Claire was talking again.

"Several times over this visit I've reminded her that you, Arthur and I are her support system and we're here to help her. And she told me we're doing a good job, and thanked us. But," my sister concluded, "I have a feeling we're going to be doing more praying throughout this process."

Yes, indeed.

IN NEW JERSEY, I made arrangements for the August trip. What could we do with the Explorer, the first brand new car Mom had ever owned? It wasn't brand new any more, but it still had some miles left. I kept thinking that my daughter and her husband could use a better vehicle than the beloved rattletrap they currently drove. I wrote to ask Mom, "Would you consider letting Rebekah and Josh have your car? Theirs is really old, and you won't need yours in California." She wrote briefly to say yes. I was left to guess how she felt about this idea because her emails were getting shorter and plainer all the time. I wondered if she'd remember giving permission. I'd just have to cross that bridge when I came to it.

TEXAS AGAIN

In August, I was back at Mom's, performing triage on her possessions. As I dug through drawers and closets, boxing things up, Mom lowered herself gingerly onto the bed to watch. I wanted her to decide which things she would take, but she rarely voiced an opinion. At length, she remarked, "You know, I really appreciate ya'll -the three of you- taking care of all this for me."

"You're very welcome," I smiled, and hauled myself up from the floor to give her an awkward hug. "I know this is hard for you."

She nodded. "You know I've been independent all my life, and it's hard to accept help. But everything'll work out. You'd have to deal with all my stuff anyway eventually, so why not now?"

Warmed by this exchange, I bent to my task with fresh

vigor. It's good to clear out the old, to make way for new or better things. Mom was trying, and I was grateful.

SAVED?

When Claire and I were children, the only acceptable reason for skipping church was a verifiable illness, preferably with vomiting. But Mom stopped attending shortly after she moved to Temple. When I asked her why, she said she didn't know anybody there. I couldn't convince her that if she began to attend, she would eventually know people there.

Mom's refusal to attend church both puzzled and concerned me. I had always assumed she was a born-again Christian. Didn't she take us to church and buy us Bibles when we were kids? But now, taking a fresh look at her lifestyle, I began to reconsider. Sure, salvation is a free gift to those who believe in Jesus. But even the devil believes in God. Good deeds don't earn a place in heaven, but the Apostle James points out that "faith without works is dead." Good works, such as helping the poor and attending church, are evidence of true faith. And if I'm reading my

Bible right, it's possible to think you're okay with God when you're not. Did Mom fall into that category? How could I know?

Mom imposed church on me when I was too young to resist, but now I went because I wanted to. This morning I was going to worship at The Vine, a church I'd never attended on any of my previous visits. Driving there, I mentally replayed a conversation Mom and I had had several years before about her conversion experience.

"Well," she said, "Every Sunday the preacher went on and on about salvation, and told us to come up to the front and get saved. People always asked me if I'd gone up front. They pestered and pestered me. So I finally just went up there to get 'em off my back."

This was not the Damascus road experience I was expecting, or even the little-white-church-in-the-valley reminiscence she might have shared. Horrified, I blurted out, "How do you know you're really saved, if you just did it to get people off your back?"

"Well, I believe now," she replied. "I believe in Jesus. Doesn't that make me saved?"

Well…. yes. But wasn't there more to it than that?

THE VINE

The Vine's website said it was "a group of imperfect people striving to be rooted in God, growing in Christ, and reaching the World." The decor was all cool colors and clean lines, and there was coffee. The worship time was lively, and the people were smiling. Better still, there was a fellowship luncheon after the service, and I was invited. Why not? My offer of kitchen help was snapped up by Zoe, an energetic woman who was clearly in charge. Soon I was transferring salad greens from boxes to bowls, and adding vegetables.

OVER THE MEAL Zoe introduced me to others at her table. They served food to each other, and engaged in a sort of gentle teasing as they ate, as people often do when their relationship has cycled repeatedly through its stages over years. Zoe, an environmental engineer, offered recycling tips and recommended a property manager for Mom's house. I watched as they all rose at once and cleaned up in tandem after the meal.

~

ON THE WAY back to the house, I wondered afresh where Mom stood with God. I believed, not in heaven, exactly -- not as it's traditionally conceived with clouds and harps-- but in eternal life with Jesus. I wanted to see Mom alive again in the new earth promised in the book of Revelation. How could I have assurance of her salvation? If she wasn't saved now, what could I do about it? Mentally, it appeared, that train had left the station. *Lord*, I prayed, *I know it's probably too late, but somehow, somehow, can you show me whether or not Mom is really saved?*

~

BACK AT THE HOUSE, I found her resting. I bent myself to purging and packing. Arthur would be here in a few days to load up Mom and her stuff in a truck and drive her to California, and I wanted to be ready.

VISITING BOBBIE AND LOU

The next morning, I took Mom to visit her sisters. Bobbie and Lou lived together, two retired old ladies in a rambling house off County Road 109. This might be the last time Mom would see Lou, because neither of them would get on a plane.

We drove over dirt roads winding through fields of corn and sorghum, stopping to open and close the padlocked gates. Cattle and horses raised their heads lazily in the glaring sun and stared at the Explorer bumping down the rutted driveway. We went through a second locked gate in a fence which encircled the house, a simple two-story dwelling fronted by a shady porch. By August, the sun had burned away the wild bluebonnets and Indian paintbrush, but Bobbie had planted golden columbine and lantana flowers along the front walkway.

In the cool, dark parlor, we talked of the weather and old movies. Neither of the aunts had seen any movies recently. Lou perched on an ottoman in a shadowy area of the room and didn't say much. She had lost weight, and her hair was gathered into a ponytail in greasy strings along her skull. I briefly recalled her red hair carefully curled and teased into a bouffant, her false lashes and red lipstick, the way she was always ready with a wickedly funny rejoinder. When had she turned into this silent person huddled in the corner like a sparrow poised to fly?

Lou had accumulated a stunning collection of rhinestone jewelry. I invited myself into the inner sanctum of her room and politely oohed and aahed over dozens of drawers and shoeboxes full of carefully-organized necklaces, bracelets, earrings and rings, wondering, *Why?* Lou never went out anymore. While Bobbie tended her plants or played with her grandchildren, Lou stayed in her room in faded pajamas, organizing jewelry components. The last time I visited, she was stringing beads onto a wire while oldies played on a dust-covered boombox. And she wasn't wearing a single piece of jewelry.

Bobbie was excited about a nest of baby owls she'd found recently. After lunch, she invited me into the yard to see the new rose bushes and little tomato plants. Out in the sunshine, crouched in the dirt to examine the seedlings, I remembered Granny, who cultivated her tiny garden plot by the side of the house as carefully as if it had been an acre. Oh, those tomatoes! You could never get flavor like that at a supermarket. Granny's garden, small as it was, taught me that there was goodness in the soil, goodness that could be coaxed up and distilled and sliced onto a plate, and eaten with the sun still in it. These, and peaches warm and juicy from the tree, testified that even a poor person, with patience and diligence, could eat like a king.

As I drove Mom home, I told her I'd like to go to a meeting at the Vine Church that evening. There was to be a meal of African specialties, and a speaker just back from Tanzania.

And I did. The food was authentic and good. Michael and Dorris excitedly shared their ten- to fifteen-year plan to create a place where abandoned babies could get food, medical care and education. Dorris, a wiry lady whose strawberry bangs brushed the tops of red plastic eyeglass frames, told me she was sixty-nine years old. I had guessed fifty-five.

At nearly seventy years old, Dorris was making a ten- to fifteen-year plan. She added, "We're not special people or anything. We aren't that smart or talented or rich. We're just doing what God has called us to do, and He is blessing."

I made a mental note to keep doing what God called me to do.

PAPER AND PLASTIC

*T*he next morning, God called me to sort, pack, and discard. I'd been dreading the paperwork, but it had to be addressed. My mother, who for years faithfully balanced her checkbook, paid her bills on time, and kept track of all her accounts, now kept bank statements in plastic grocery bags on the floor of her walk-in closet. On a previous visit I had laboriously set up a filing system, labeling each folder with company logos cut from return envelopes, hoping the visual cues would help her stay on top of things. They didn't.

I opened the closet door, surveyed the mayhem, and shuddered. I lowered myself to the floor and began sorting papers, trying not to scowl. Mom never actually told me my face would freeze like that, but there was no sense risking it. I made a pile of papers for each account: utility bills, financial statements, receipts, medical records. She kept it all.

Mom couldn't lower herself to the floor, but she hovered, finally lying on her bed to watch me. "Are you throwing those ones away?" she asked, furrowing her brow.

"Yes, these go in the trash."

"I heard you're not supposed to put financial papers in the trash. People can steal it and get your personal information."

"That's okay. These are just the advertising parts of the mailings. There's no personal information on them. And the ones that do have information, I'm tearing off that part," I explained, holding up a paper and demonstrating.

"Do they have my signature on them?"

"I don't think so." *Why would her signature be on mailings?*

"They do have my address, though."

"Yes, they do."

"I think we should tear off the part that has the address."

I had an idea. I asked, "You have a shredder, don't you?" She did.

So I set her up with the shredder and gave her all superfluous documents. It could only handle a few papers at a time, but Mom was content to shred away every imagined evidence of her personal information, making her trash impervious to thieves.

That night, while Mom checked her email, I made a hasty run-through of the kitchen cabinets, removing unrecyclable items. I slunk out into the darkness and quietly slid them into the trash bin on the curb. The town only picked up one container of trash and one of recycling twice a week, and we had a lot. I would need to fill both bins every time, or I'd be forced to make a run to the dump later. I noiselessly collected empty yogurt tubs, glass jars, cans of baked beans with years-past expiration dates, and separated Oil of Olay. She hated to waste things.

FINDING MONEY

The next morning Mom hobbled into the kitchen and found me eating breakfast. She said, as if charging me with wrongdoing, "You just *dive* right in, don't you?"

She thought I was always eating. Compared to her, I was.

Making another sortie, she asked, "What are you eating?" On the table in front of me sat a box of cereal, a carton of milk and a bowl with cereal and milk in it. There stood my mother, ninety pounds of flaccid flesh and bones, playing her old game of goad-and-retreat. For once, I was rendered speechless. She laughed. "You mean you don't even know what you're having for breakfast?"

To keep from saying something sarcastic, I shoveled another spoonful of cereal into my mouth. Just when she seemed harmless, she'd pull out the old weapons and take a random swipe at me, just for old time's sake.

Culling through more things that day, I found $300 cash in a metal box. Maybe I'd hand this to Arthur for use on the road. He was to arrive that afternoon, and begin packing up the UHaul. Zoe had found us a strong high school student to help with loading. Tomorrow Arthur would bundle Mom up into the cab of a fifteen-foot truck, and they'd set out for California. I would stay till the end of August, finishing the job.

Pawing through Mom's paperwork, I found more accounts than expected. How many of these were still active? What a mess. Claire had power of attorney, but I didn't, so I'd have to cart Mom to the bank. She'd have to sit and stand more than she liked, but it couldn't be helped.

As we sat in the lobby, Mom looked through her purse. She pulled out a card and asked, "What is this?"

"That's your AAA membership card."

"Do you think I should keep it?"

I examined the card more closely. "Well, it's expired, and you probably won't need it in California. So you can throw that away."

"What's this one?"

"That's your military ID," I explained. She has had one of these ever since she married my father fifty-four years ago.

"Should I keep that or throw it away?"

"Definitely keep that. You need it for your widow's benefits."

Next she showed me her membership card to the YMCA in California, dated 2001. Had she really once been a member of the YMCA? She said, "I don't want to throw this away. I might use it."

She was so small, hunched next to me. I was almost afraid the people in the bank would see her brain oozing out her ear. I put my arm around her and whispered, "Maybe we can work on this later, at home."

The bank officer discovered that Mom had a CD with a balance of $10,000. Another had $35,000. At another bank, I discovered more accounts Mom had forgotten. How much more cash was floating around out there with Mom's name on it?

HAVE CHERRY PASTRIES,
WILL TRAVEL

That afternoon Arthur arrived. In his usual man-with-a-mission mode, he had picked up the truck before he even arrived at the house, and he and Zoe's young friend loaded it. Later that evening, Bobbie came to say goodbye. Behind Mom's closed bedroom door, Arthur and I heard a cloudburst of weeping. After Bobbie left, Mom shuffled into the living room, blew her nose and muttered, "I'm sorry," presumably for her unseemly display of emotion.

We had waited for this day, but it felt sudden and over-whelming. A game of Rummikub got us all back into familiar territory.

THE FOLLOWING MORNING all three of us were up early. Mom surprised me by taking a shower, something she hadn't done, to my knowledge, the entire week I'd been there.

~

My sister's husband was not like any other man of my acquaintance. The prospect of driving a seven-ton vehicle halfway across the United States with a frail old woman was to him neither a daunting challenge nor an onerous duty. Rather, he regarded it as a challenge to be manfully met, like slaying a dragon or chopping a cord of firewood. Arthur was tall enough, but the force of his personality made him seem bigger somehow, like a character in a Dickens novel. His voice could fill a room, and he employed it often, as he was persistently in good spirits and ready to give any topic a thorough going-over. He was eager to get going. Today especially, I was glad to have him on our team.

When all was ready, Arthur carefully lifted Mom onto the passenger seat. She reached down and patted the bag of cherry pastries between her feet. And off they went. He would be taking her in and out of that seat dozens of times, for potty stops and food stops and hotel stays. I sent up a prayer for both of them. I then turned afresh to the boxes, this time with no distractions and no stopping to explain why I ate food several times a day.

GOD ANSWERS

1979

*A*s a child, I watched a lot of nature shows on television. One memorable episode featured the bowerbird, notable for its extraordinary courtship behavior. To attract a mate, the male painstakingly constructs an elaborate leafy shelter and lines its entrance with anything he can find that is colorful, bright, or shiny. This might include rocks or moss or flowers, foil, or bits of plastic or glass. Ginny, like the bowerbird, enjoyed bling. Not to wear or to use, or even to look at. She just acquired it. What impulse drove my mother, and Aunt Lou, to continue buying and storing costume jewelry? Here it all was, in boxes and drawers and suitcases and bags, staring up at me. And I had no idea what to do with it all. Rings, necklaces, bracelets and, especially, pins. Who wears pins?

I went through old papers and housewares. There was a tire, a mini-fridge, oil paints, house paints, TVs, monitors and other electronics, and batteries. It's as if my mother thought, *What random and pointless items can I collect that will require several complicated steps for their proper disposal?* Fortunately, I had Zoe's cell number. She had connections, and in short order she sent someone from the city to pick it all up for recycling.

Sorting through the remnants of Mom's life, I felt increasingly irritable. Why did she make lists of books she read, puzzles she created or worked, pictures she cut out or painted or drew, videotapes of soap operas and movies. Apparently, my mother spent the last half of her life as a consumer. If she produced anything, it benefited nobody, or very few people, and probably none in a meaningful way. She collected and consumed till the very end, and had nothing, really, to show for it. Was I being harsh? It felt strange and wrong to judge the way my mother spent her time. But it looked to me like she had wasted a lot of it.

If my kids cleared out my house in thirty years, I wondered, would they find evidence of a life well spent? Or would they examine my artifacts and shake their heads?

As I worked, I began to reconsider. I wondered if Mom's shrinking world was a cause or a result of her choices. Her body had suffered from lack of nourishment. Isn't it true of the mind and spirit as well? Don't we thrive when we give and serve? Was I just projecting my issues onto Mom? Hoarding anything, whether literal money or goods, or one's heart and gifts, paradoxically impoverishes. But sharing makes a person rich.

I thought, *I must remember these things.*

I came across many ancient but unused items: sheets,

shampoo, toothbrushes, single-blade razors, a Walkman. There was a tape recording of my high school choir.

And then I found this letter, dated July 24,1979, addressed to her brother John. It was on two pieces of translucent onionskin paper, typed on Mom's IBM Selectric. Of all the letters she wrote over the years, why did she keep a copy of this one? She was responding to a letter he wrote about the breakup of his marriage.

Ginny told her little brother that the Bible is a limitless source of information. She recommended the Living Bible paraphrase and offered to get one for him. She exhorted him to lean on Jesus because "when you have him with you, you are never alone again."

Ginny told John:

```
I am ashamed to say that I've not given my
testimony often enough to have it polished, but
I will say that ever since I was seventeen and
accepted Christ, I've never known what it feels
like to be completely alone. Even during those
years I strayed away from Him and His church, He
was still ready to take me back and I can see now
that my life would have been completely
different had I not gone through those years of
trying to "go my own way." It was during that
time I made the important decision to marry and
went ahead with it without praying or seeking
His will for my life. As a result, I find myself
married twenty-one years to a non-Christian.


Fortunately, he's never objected to my church
doings and goings nor the way I raised our
girls to be Christian-oriented, but how lovely
```

it would be to have a husband who'd be by our
side at Sunday services, etc.

So that was what happened. I didn't make that mistake.
No --my ex and I agree-- the mistakes came later.

She went on to say:

When a person "worships" anything else except
God, then he's never happy, even while he's
wondering why he's not happy.

Well, John, no doubt you don't welcome a sermon
from me and I didn't mean for this to be one. I am
writing for only one reason --because I love
you and want to help you all I can.

I could hardly believe it. Here, amongst this gargantuan
pile of junk was the hard evidence I craved, my mother's
adult testimony, with evidence of repentance, written and
inexplicably stored twenty-three years before I needed it.
Alone in that big house, I laughed like a hyena. I could
hardly wait to tell Claire.

TWO ROOMS BELOW THE TRACKS

SEPTEMBER 2012
VISTA, CALIFORNIA

*A*rthur and Ginny arrived in Vista, a sunny town north of San Diego a few miles from the beach. Arthur reported to Claire, and Claire reported to me, that Mom ate almost nothing but cherry pastries on the trip. "Arthur did his best. He took her to decent restaurants, but he couldn't *make* her eat," she sighed. Once again, I was exhausted, stretched out on the guest bed, phone pressed to my ear. Soon the bed would be donated to a worthy charity.

~

THAT DAY, I cleaned out the fridge in preparation for selling it. I threw out all the old food, and wiped up spilled Dr. Pepper and milk, old lettuce leaves, sticky ketchup. I was sick of *stuff*. I was tired of cleaning. I resolved to seriously declutter when I got home.

But my mother's family was poor even before the Depression. She was always haunted by the specter of Not Enough.

Once, Mom showed me a photograph of the home in which she spent her early years. A friend had visited Ballinger and taken a picture of it. "I'm surprised it's still standing!" she exclaimed. "It was nothing but a shack even back then." And she was right. Bobbie calls this house "two rooms below the tracks." Meaning, they lived on the poor side of town, among "the colored folks." It was two rooms, not two bedrooms. Two rooms in which to cook, eat, sleep, talk, do laundry, play, and study. Two rooms for six people.

"If you wanted to take a bath," my mother told me, when she still had memories, "you had to fill the big kettle with water, heat it up on the stove, and fill the big metal washtub with enough water to make it warm. Then, you had to tell everybody to get out of that room, which was both kitchen and bedroom, and they had to either go outside or into the other room. And *then* you had to hope that nobody came in while you were bathing."

Then the day came when Ginny had two bathrooms, and three bedrooms, a kitchen and dining room all to herself. How she must have relished her privacy here! Soon new people would make fresh impressions on the space where Mom enjoyed autonomy, and the Texas weather she loved, for ten years. I took one last look around, locked up and climbed into the Explorer for the drive to Rebekah and Josh's.

TWO ROOMS AT OMNIA

*O*mnia offered "a uniquely vibrant living experience with innovative accommodations." How can accommodations be innovative? If they would just give assistance as needed, I'd be happy.

~

BACK IN NEW JERSEY, I got a message from Claire:

```
Yesterday was the first day since Mom has
moved to Omnia that I didn't need to go over
there. I aim to get to the point where all
can be taken care of if I go over there once
or twice a week.
```

She said she felt moody, and I found myself unaccountably irritable. Moody and irritable were not what we were going for when we moved Mom.

How did we not see this coming? Mom's life was disintegrating, and chunks of it were tumbling through the cracks. We were picking up a few bits here and there. It was like she was trying to carry too many sacks of groceries, and was dropping them, and we eventually noticed and stopped to lend a hand. And suddenly now we were holding Mom's entire grocery order in our hands, in addition to our own bags and boxes, looking at each other wide-eyed, staggering under the weight of it all and trying not to drop the eggs. Could we do this? And we didn't even dare to voice the question, *What if it gets harder?*

ASSISTANCE, PLEASE

AUTUMN 2012

*T*here was so much we assumed Mom was doing for herself. Now it fell to Claire. There must be, we reasoned, some tasks we could delegate. Could we pay someone to drive her to appointments? Did Claire have to provide *everything* except laundry, meals and the dispensing of meds, which Omnia was supposed to do?

And what could I do, so far away?

One day Claire wrote,

Today I was out walking, and listening to a sermon. The speaker said, 'Just because you've had a bad week doesn't mean God doesn't love you.' I almost burst into tears right out in the street! He said that serving God amidst pain is the only way that we can really know that we love Him. The pain I feel lately is because we have lost our old Mom. The change in her is ever before me now.

Wow. In our family, we don't even cry in the living room, much less on the street. I responded:

```
It costs you a great deal to sacrifice for Mom,
and she can't appreciate it. God is the only one
who really knows the nature and depth of our
sacrifices. I imagine them rising up like smoke,
a soothing aroma in His nostrils.
```

I felt like a smarmy hypocrite. After typing these words, I pushed away from the desk and stood, gazing vacantly out the window. My second floor walkup looked out over the parking lot of Our Lady of Lourdes Catholic Church. This empty vista, a rarity in crowded northern New Jersey, afforded an open view of the sky. On clear days, even cold ones, the sunlight slanted through the picture window and flooded the room with light and warmth. The red oak out front was just beginning to turn, the promise of another mellow New Jersey autumn. I sighed and paced the length of the living room. When I moved into this apartment, I hated the dated cut-pile carpet and the dark wood window- and door-frames. Now it felt like a refuge, an aerie from which I could coolly observe the world outside.

It was easy to send encouraging words, but I wasn't the one doing the work. I had thought we could entrust Mom's care to professionals. I had thought the assisted living facility would render more... assistance.

Did I weigh my expectations, before we undertook to move Mom? Did I really think about how it would go?

We'd put our mom into a safe, healthy, clean and

pleasant place. *But...* we couldn't protect her from herself. We didn't factor in the dementia, the inevitable downward trajectory.

We were powerless to make her to eat. We were incapable of giving her friends. We were unable to make a life for her. There are some things a person can only do for herself. But what if a person just can't do them anymore?

The truth must be faced. Mom's health and brain function would never improve. I sat back down at the computer and typed out a message to my sister. I told her that this was a time God had given us to strengthen our faith, exercising it like a muscle. Claire agreed, but confessed,

```
I feel personally responsible for Mom's
happiness, and that's not a reasonable
expectation to place on myself. She doesn't
expect it. Please pray for me to take every
thought captive to obey Jesus; my fretting is
not helping anyone, and in my rational mind that
is very easy to see.
```

My fretting about Claire wouldn't help either. She'd clearly gotten the short end of the stick. Hypocrite or not, I could only offer a listening ear, encouragement, and occasional visits. This year, my schedule was more crowded than ever. I had a full course load of online college classes and a Bible class for Chinese students. I was on the board of directors at church. Michael was taking a Spanish class at a community college, where I was to drive him twice a week. Also, he decided that in his last year of high school he would add speech and debate to his already-knee-wobblingly full schedule of chorale, men's ensemble, choir, and just plain old academics. For now, Claire would have to fill in the gaps where Omnia failed, and I would have to stand on the sidelines, shouting out encouragements from three thousand miles east.

THINKING AHEAD

*W*hile Mom's world had contracted to the present and immediate, Claire and I constantly thought ahead. She was homeschooling Joel, who would graduate that spring. She and Arthur had put their Tennessee cabin on the market, anticipating a quick sale and a financial infusion. And when she heard that Mom had "peed her pants" during the night, Claire's mind immediately leapt to a future of nightly accidents. She told me, "I found out there's a whole branch of medicine called urodynamics."

It made peeing sound like an exciting game of skill and chance.

BLOSSOM AND DECLINE

DECEMBER 2012
VISTA, CALIFORNIA

*W*hile Claire explored the uncharted territory of urinary incontinence, I was overseeing Michael's final year of high school. While still taking my own online classes, I drove him to activities, created a transcript, and helped with college applications. Next year would be different. After twenty-two years of homeschooling, I would just be working on my own Bachelor's degree. How many more car trips would I make with Michael, talking, sharing music, laughing? How many more times would I overhear those hilarious exchanges with his friends in the back seat? How much longer would I be able to share an illuminating portion of my anthropology text, or just explain something I thought he needed to know? Could a person feel joy and grief at the same time? I wanted to keep this life. But it was fast draining away, and a new, more somber life seemed ever closer.

People are born and grow like plants; they blossom and decline. As my mother was descending into confusion and dependency, Michael and Joel were reaching greater heights of knowledge and independence. I decided that instead of just feeling bad about Mom, I would feel happy for the boys, too. I figured, it may not affect their lives at all, but it would help me keep my balance.

AT LAST, I CAN HELP. A LITTLE.

JANUARY 2013
CALIFORNIA/NEW JERSEY

*M*y mother never had many friends. But there were a few who sent Christmas cards. Mom remembered their names, and that they were friends -- but nothing more. She thought Claire should write them to explain what's happened to her.

"But I haven't had time even to send more than one Christmas card of my own," Claire protested. "Would you address the envelopes? You could just copy the return addresses from the Christmas cards you've received."

"I don't write," Mom countered.

"But you write when you do your crosswords."

"Oh, that's not writing."

I told Claire to send me the envelopes, and I would write to Mom's old friends. Here, at last, was something I could do.

FALLING

*Y*ou think it's hard to climb up, but then you realize that going down is even harder. When I was about twelve years old, I went rock climbing with friends. On the descent, I hit a patch of scree and realized with rising terror that the incline was sharper than I thought. I was suddenly in slow motion, going down too fast and powerless to stop. Sometimes I recalled this feeling when I got messages and phone calls from Claire.

My sister kept hoping Mom would at least plateau, but the declivity just got steeper. Our mother lay in her bed, made plaintive calls to Claire, and wouldn't eat. The doctor offered to prescribe a feeding tube, but Claire said Mom would balk at that. I would balk, if it were me. It was clear we would be making more and more decisions for her, and we needed some sort of guide. My sister asked me to get Mom's responses on a document called "The Five Wishes," which indicates how a person wants to be treated if they become terminally ill. I told her I would try.

DO NOT RESUSCITATE

SEPTEMBER 2002
LAKE FOREST, CALIFORNIA

I wish we'd had the Five Wishes, or something like it, for Dad.

In 2002, when Mom and Dad lived in California, Dad fought prostate cancer, but it eventually colonized his body and left him immobile and in agony. The hospice set him up with a morphine patch and a hospital bed in the living room.

One day when I was there, the hospice nurse came for a visit. After checking on Dad, she sat down with Mom at the kitchen table. From her briefcase she pulled out a piece of paper called a DNR ("Do Not Resuscitate") order, and gently pressed Mom to sign it. She explained that if paramedics were called, they would be legally obligated to spare no effort to revive Dad. They might have to perform CPR, which could break his ribs. If there were a DNR in place, Dad would be allowed to expire naturally without such trauma.

I never knew CPR could break somebody's ribs. But cancer in the bones renders them as fragile as sidewalk chalk.

After the nurse left, Mom sat there for a long time with her elbows on the table, palms pressed to her forehead. Finally, she pulled herself up and approached Dad. She stood by his bedside and explained everything, holding the paper up for him to see. Over and over she said, "Keith, I need you to tell me what to do. I don't know what to do. They want me to sign this order for them not to resuscitate you if your heart stops. Is that what you want?" He hadn't spoken a word for weeks. He just stared at her. My father, who in better days had a keen and instant grasp on matters others found opaque, could make no reply.

She turned to me in tears. "Susan, if I sign this paper, it feels like I'm signing his death warrant."

"You know Dad better than anyone," I told her. "What would the old, pre-cancer Dad say?"

She stood for a minute, silent. "I think he would say I should sign it."

My father had always been the calm voice of reason. Now I heard my own voice, calm and rational, saying, "Then that's what you should do."

I felt, in that moment, I was standing up for him. He was, as far as I knew, an atheist and a materialist. He also wanted to live. Only four weeks ago he had told me, as we were sorting through his possessions, "You know, Susan,

I'll probably never get out of this bed. But if I do, I'd like to know I still have my sleeping bag if I want to go camping."

Hope against hope. So human. But Dad was looking up at us like that now, in his cancer-riddled body, unable to think or speak. Now he had to trust Mom. I couldn't bear the thought of paramedics crashing through the door and pumping his fragile sternum in a vain attempt to restart his faltering heart. He wouldn't want that.

She signed it, and wept. I cried, too, later that night, as I lay in my old bed in my old room. A few weeks later, when Dad's heart fluttered to a stop, we were all there, Mom, Claire and I, clustered around that bed. No paramedics and no trauma.

GINNY'S WISHES

*N*ow I was on the phone with Mom, asking whether she wanted CPR, a feeding tube or antibiotics if she were terminally ill. It was awkward at first, but after I explained she was all cooperation. Soon all the blanks were filled in. She said that if there were any chance she'd get better, she wanted treatments. If she were close to death, she didn't want life-support treatment. She didn't want a feeding tube, or intravenous fluids, or CPR.

There was a section in The Five Wishes which allows the patient to indicate "I wish to be massaged with warm oils as often as I can be." Up to this point, Mom had murmured her consent to cool, moist cloths, warm baths, medicine for pain control, and music, but she stopped short at massage oils. "Susan," she began, as if to lecture me. "I have lived my entire life up till now without being massaged with warm oils. I think I'll be *just fine* without that." I could almost see her on the other end of the line, drawing herself up with dignity. Massage oils, to her, seemed somewhat naughty.

Well, that was easier than I thought. It was more like a road map than a legal document, but I felt better.

DIAGNOSIS: ALZHEIMER'S

MARCH 2013
VISTA, CALIFORNIA

That winter, Dr. Szabo, Mom's new neurologist, said it looked like she had Alzheimer's disease. He told Claire, "If you can go to sleep at night knowing that your mother is safe and secure, then you're doing a good job as a daughter." Thank God for Dr. Szabo. Claire needed to hear this.

Michael would spend the summer with me in New Jersey, but in August he'd be going off to college in Pennsylvania. I could work on my degree anywhere, so after all the graduation madness was over, I made plans to go to California for weeks at a time and give Claire a break.

DELIRIUM

*B*ut before graduation madness, there was wedding madness. Tomorrow Claire and Arthur's older son Jesse was to marry his sweetheart, Dinae, at an oh-so-trendy hipster venue in Los Angeles. We were all looking forward to a lovely afternoon of drought-tolerant greenery, chalkboard signage, and drinks served in Mason jars at burly tables of unfinished wood. How many bushy-bearded young men would be there, I wondered, and would they be wearing those ridiculous-looking skinny jeans?

Mom couldn't attend the wedding, so on my way from the airport I dropped by to see her. After the wedding there would be time for more leisurely visits. There she was, lying on her bed, as usual, propped up with pillows, and doing a crossword puzzle.

"Well, hello!" she exclaimed. Of course, she forgot I was coming, so my visit was a delightful surprise.

"I'm here for Jesse's wedding," I smiled.

"I dish I could know, but I'm just sitting here drinking my pooper."

I glanced at Claire, who looked quizzically at me. We made an excuse to go into the next room.

"Is she always this bad?" I asked in an undertone.

"Well, she doesn't always make sense, but this is really weird," exclaimed Claire. "Let me call the nurse."

The nurse theorized that Mom had a urinary tract infection and needed antibiotics.

"I've had urinary tract infections, and I didn't talk nonsense," I asserted.

"It's different in the elderly," he explained. "It sometimes affects their mood and mental state. It can cause delirium."

Mom was delirious, all right. She went on and on, only occasionally making sense. She got up to show us something on the computer, and grabbed onto the bed and the dresser to make her way laboriously across the room.

"Um...Mom, you should use your walker for that," I reminded her.

"Oh, yes, that thinger. I can't know that too. Have it there? Never mind."

I resolved to do something as soon as I returned from the wedding, to keep her from falling and breaking her one good hip.

NO MORE HIPS LEFT TO BREAK

*T*he wedding was a success. And Mom's limbs remained intact, such as they were.

Claire and I took our mother to lunch, and to see her new doctor. We said goodbye and left, chatting in earnest on our way down the stairs to Omnia's big front entrance. As we passed the reception desk, an alarm clanged on the second floor. It might have been anything, really, in this building full of elderly people, but something told me *hold up*. We heard rapid footsteps above, and I asked the receptionist what happened. Recognizing Claire and me, she said, "Oh, it's your mother! Your mother rang the emergency bell."

It's probably a mistake, I thought, as we raced back up the stairs. There was Mom in the hallway, on the floor just outside her apartment. I ran to her and threw myself over her body, as if to keep her warm. "We're here, Mom. Claire and I are right here."

She was all apologies. She was practically in tears. She didn't know how she fell. She said she was clumsy. "It's okay, Mom. You're not clumsy. It's okay," we told her.

Young, burly paramedics came and took her to the Emergency Room. In the ambulance, Mom murmured, "I have a confession to make."

I leaned forward and whispered, "What is it?"

Her eyes widened, and she whispered back, as if to scandalize me, "I bite my fingernails."

An x-ray revealed a broken hip. Sitting in the hospital's waiting area, I wondered if Mom would live through hip-replacement surgery. I knew she would never walk again. She wouldn't, or couldn't, learn anything new. Or even sort of new.

NOTHING IS NORMAL

APRIL 2013
NEW JERSEY/CALIFORNIA

*M*om made it through the surgery, and was discharged into Alta Loma, a skilled nursing facility where she was supposed to learn to walk again. I found her sitting up in bed watching television. I hugged her and asked, "Did you have physical therapy this morning?"

She replied, "*I* don't know," as if it were impossible for her to have this information.

Perhaps this was a poor question. I tried again. "How are you feeling?"

"This is a godawful place."

My mother had never used language like that before. She added irritably, "I can't get anyone to *help* me."

"Have you been using your button?"

She frowned and wrinkled her nose. "My *what?*"

"Your call button." I showed her the device like a small flashlight hooked onto the bed rail. It had a large red button on the end. "When you need help, push this button and someone will come and help you." I demonstrated.

When the attendant appeared, I asked if Mom could get out of bed. "Sure," she said. "We want patients to move around as much as they can."

"Can we put my mother in a wheelchair and maybe I can take her around the grounds?"

Of course we could. I took her around to see the flowers and trees, and we heard the birds sing. "It's a beautiful day," I said.

Mom sighed. "Nothing seems normal anymore."

"I think we'd better go in now," I said. "I think it's just about time for dinner."

"That's another thing. How do you know what time it is?"

"I look at my watch."

She seemed skeptical. "What I really want is frozen yogurt."

At least now she was making sense. I took her back to her room and carefully eased her back into bed. Pulling the rail firmly into place, I remarked, "Remember, when you need help, ring your bell."

"What bell? I don't have a bell."

I showed it to her again, and again she was surprised.

Dementia is a deceptive disease. It robs bits of this and chunks of that, but leaves some things untouched. Mom could chatter politely with the staff at Alta Loma, just like she made small talk with sales clerks thirty years ago. But she couldn't remember the bell.

I pulled out of the parking lot, thinking, *Why do I feel so relaxed?* Then I remembered Mom's bed had rails, so for the first time in a long time, I wasn't worried she'd fall.

HONOR THY MOTHER

I flew back to New Jersey, to prepare for the end-of-school-year frenzy of practices and parties. For the time being Mom was safe and cared for, and the insurance was paying. We'd been granted a six-week reprieve.

While Mom was in rehab, not rehabilitating, her apartment at Omnia was waiting for her. But she needed something more.

Arthur had already visited three "memory care" units, the locked-down areas for people with dementia. "It's terrible," he declared. "The residents are all herded together. The employees don't interact with them. Everybody looks scared. They don't get exposed to sunlight or trees. And I went to what are supposedly the best facilities in the area. I wouldn't put anyone in there," he declared, shaking his head, "unless I were sure that they had no mental capacity at all. Then they wouldn't perceive how depressing it is."

Arthur saw the positive side of everything, but he could say only one good thing about memory care. "At least they won't get lost or hit by a car in there, or burn the place down."

I thought, *Maybe I should just set up housekeeping somewhere nearby, move Mom in with me, and take care of her myself.* Leaving her with strangers felt like abandoning her. But was I strong enough to care for Mom?

The people I asked about this idea gushed about the benefits to the patient, but tiptoed carefully around the cost to the caregiver. No one wanted to discourage me from doing my absolute best for Mom. But they didn't want to come right out and say, "Yeah, caregiving is like putting your heart, and sometimes your body, through a meat grinder." Instead, they said things like, "Make sure you know what you're getting into." They just didn't tell me what, exactly, I was getting into.

How much longer would she live? If I knew it were only a matter of months, like it was with Dad, I might put all my effort into making her last days as pleasant as possible. But this could last for years. I just didn't know if I had it in me.

I was so scared when Dad was sick. I was afraid to be with him, and afraid to not be with him. For reasons I still don't understand, I had prayed to be at his bedside when he died. And though I lived three thousand miles away at the time, I saw him breathe his last. I had prayed for closure, and I got it. Would God hear and answer my prayers this time? Because I wanted to do what was right for Mom, and for all of us.

Jesus said, "If you ask Me anything in My name, I will do it." This, followed by, "If you love Me, you will keep My commandments." If I was trying to keep the commandment to honor my mother, and if I asked Jesus to give me what I needed to do it, how could He *not* help me?

AZURE SKIES

MAY 2013

A local friend suggested Azure Skies, the newest and most innovative memory care facility in the area. It was danged expensive, but I thought we should move Mom straight there from Alta Loma. At this hectic time of year, phone conversations were a luxury, but Claire called to ask why Mom would be better off at Azure Skies than Omnia.

"Okay," I began. "Let's consider how she would do at Omnia. Even before the fall, she had a hard time walking. She holds onto furniture or walls, and she has no depth perception, so she sometimes misses. And now we don't know whether she'll ever be able to walk on her own again."

"Right," said Claire. "She's had mobility problems for a while."

"Okay, here's what I think would happen at Omnia.

She'll lie in bed all day and do nothing. She won't walk, because it hurts. She won't remember how to use the computer, TV, or phone. She won't do any puzzles or read any books. She won't go down for meals and she won't drink water. She'll get dehydrated and get more urinary tract infections. She won't eat meals, but she'll ask for frozen yogurt and chocolates."

There was a gusty sigh on the other end of the line.

I continued, "She won't shower or brush her teeth. She may or may not remember to use her walker. She'll keep the potty by the bed, and she may or may not have success using it. Left to her own devices, she'll go down the path to wasting, dehydration and more falls. Right?"

"That's a very bleak picture."

"I know. And she needs more help to do things like brush her teeth and drink water and take a shower."

Claire said, "But when Mom first moved to Omnia, they asked if she wanted help with showering, dressing, hair grooming, and things like that. She very huffily said *no*. I didn't insist because I wanted her retain some dignity. But she *does* need help even if she doesn't want it."

"Right," I said.

"Whether she ends up at Azure Skies or Omnia, her care plan will have to reflect her current needs. What *we* know she needs, not what she thinks she needs," continued Claire. She was once again putting herself in Mom's shoes and was reluctant to take away her agency. But Mom had already lost it. It was nobody's fault. She just didn't take care of herself, and somebody had to do it.

A NEW WAY OF LOVING

$\mathscr{A}$fter weeks of futility at Alta Loma, Mom complained to Claire that she was "parked in the hallway for hours" in a wheelchair. She was tired of the noise, of taking pills, doing exercises, being interrupted. She just wanted to be left alone.

What should be done with Mom? She was no longer able to do the things she liked, and now she had to do things she didn't like, just when she was losing the emotional capacity to handle such changes. I needed to talk with someone who knew about these things. My friend Valerie shepherded her mother through her final days. Valerie listened, as she always does. She told me, "You need to learn her language now. She may never speak your language again, but you'll learn her language."

What language was that? Physical presence. Physical touch. We had never been good at this. We were independent, cerebral people. We played board games, talked and wrote. We rarely hugged, and never cuddled or held hands.

But Valerie was right. I would have to learn a whole new set of skills to win this game. Instead of loving Mom with telephone calls, emails and board games, we would have to love her with hugs, hand-holding, and chocolates.

I tried to call Mom more often. One day, when she was more lucid than she had been in a while, she told me, "As bad as these last few weeks have been, they could've been a lot, lot worse."

I can't think of how they could've been worse.

"I don't know what I would do without you and Claire," said Mom, with tears in her voice. She asked me to pray for her, for "a good healing sleep," and I did, right then and there. It was the first time I'd prayed over the phone with my mother. Priceless.

SAFETY VS. FREEDOM

JUNE 2013
VISTA, CALIFORNIA

*A*s I was learning new skills, Claire was making calculations. She wrote,

```
With Mom's current income and annuities, she
could afford to pay for about 10 years of Azure
Skies before even needing to touch her IRA. So
even though it's shriekingly expensive, it is a
possibility.
```

A series of pictures flashed through my mind: Ginny saving proofs of purchase to get free products, buying clothing and housewares at garage sales, complaining bitterly about inflation. She wrote on her calendar the amount of change she had picked up on her walk that day.

"Twenty-one cents," "fourteen cents," and "fifty-seven cents" are carefully penned in and circled, sometimes emphasized with an exclamation point, if the day's haul were unusually large. This child of the Great Depression rejoiced in every coin she found, no matter how small. "Some people won't stoop to pick up a penny on the street," she told me more than once, shaking her head. "Not me. I know the value of a penny."

~

WE TOOK the apartment at Azure Skies, gave Omnia notice, and made plans to move Mom again.

But how could we prevent another fall? Bed rails were allowed only if hospice authorized them. It was illegal for Azure Skies to restrain its residents in any way. It was a dilemma: Mom was entitled to freedom, but she'd lost the sense to use it. We didn't want Mom to be confined, but we didn't want her to fall again. The only solution was surveillance. Would the people at Azure Skies respond promptly to her summons? Would she even remember to use the call button?

GIVING CLAIRE A BREAK

AUGUST 2013

*I*n June I flew from Newark to San Diego again, so Claire could think of something besides Mom for a whole week.

I was eager to see how Mom was doing at the new facility. Its website claims Azure Skies is "a secure, gated community specializing in Alzheimer's care." It certainly looked grand. The handsome wood paneling, sky-blue damask lounge chairs and wrought iron chandelier shouted *opulence*. There was a grand piano in the front room, and in the rear was a stately living room area with leather couches and a working fireplace.

I pushed a button at the entrance and the heavy double doors wheezed open. Once I was inside, they slowly began to close. An elderly man, surprisingly limber, seized the opportunity to dart out. The receptionist summoned a worker to retrieve him. It reminded me of the way our cat used to lurk about the front door in hopes of escaping into the great unknown beyond.

I signed in, and the receptionist handed me a key fob which opened the elevators and exit doors. On the way to Mom's room, it was easy to distinguish residents from employees. The employees walked purposefully. The residents, though clean and neat, stood or shuffled, and they looked like they were trying to gather up the words to ask me for help.

Turning a corner of the hallway I passed the spacious dining room, bathed in sunlight. The dark wood tables stood with quiet dignity on the gleaming walnut-finish laminate flooring. There were flowers on each table, and cloth napkins were folded in pert triangles at each setting.

Mom's bed was positioned near the large window, so she could, in theory, look out on the clear blue sky and lush landscaping. We were not allowed to open the window for fresh air, however, as it would constitute a breach of security.

And we *needed* fresh air in there. Mom's potty was right next to the bed, and she kept her door closed. As I entered the room, I was hit in the face with the stink of urine.

Mom was happy to see me, as usual. After hugging her, I emptied the plastic potty bowl, wondering why nobody else had done it.

I wanted to take my mother outside. I helped her into her wheelchair and, armed with my magic fob, headed for the exit, leaving her door open to the hallway, for fresh-ish air.

Ginny's new home was situated on almost five acres of

prime North County real estate. The sidewalks encircled a lawn which was as robust and closely-clipped as a golf course. In fact, there was a putting green in the middle, a small playground area, presumably for visiting grandchildren, and a vegetable garden. We were the only ones there, though. We paused under a grapefruit tree, and I picked one of the fruits and held it up to her nose. "Isn't that a wonderful smell?" I asked.

"It doesn't smell like anything to me," she said.

I sat on a bench and peeled the fruit, pulled it into sections and carefully sucked the juice. Mom said she didn't want any.

It didn't matter what I said to Mom, as long as I was physically present. I didn't have to make sense, or think of transitions, or explain anything. I didn't have to listen to her thoughts and render a well-considered response. She had nothing to say. I, on the other hand, always had plenty to say. I rambled on about anything and nothing at all, and eventually it was time to go in.

Back in the room, someone from the kitchen brought a tray with lasagna, broccoli, garlic bread, a small green salad, and a scoop of vanilla ice cream. "Oooh," I said. "I love lasagna."

"Is that *pasta*?" Mom exclaimed, spitting out the word as if throwing back an insult. "Why do they always have to give me *pasta*? And garlic bread. Ick." She shook her head, and refused to dignify the vegetables with any response at all. She ate the ice cream, though. Before I went, she asked me for chocolates, and I left her with a bag of them.

LEAVING HOME

OCTOBER 1981/AUGUST 2013

One fall day in 1981, I loaded up my 1966 Volvo and got ready to leave.

After high school I had halfheartedly taken a few courses at a community college. But what I really wanted was to get away from my parents' home in California, to go east, to old-fashioned New England. Like one of the three little pigs, I went to seek my fortune.

In the driveway of the Lake Forest house, Mom and I embraced several times and spoke of the route, of safety, of staying in touch. She got all teary, turned abruptly and went into the house. I sighed, got behind the wheel, and drove off. I wouldn't see my mother again for several years.

She had gone into the house, she told me years later, simply to get herself some tissues. When she came out to continue her leave-taking, she could just see the Volvo turning the corner. My mother erupted in a fresh volley of tears and spent the rest of the day weeping.

But I never cried. I was eager to be on my way, to experience new sights, new smells, new relationships. I was on my own, giddy with possibilities.

I never considered how Mom felt about my leaving. I never thought of her feelings at all. She was always emoting -jesting or seething or griping or laughing. Claire and I joked that she cried at supermarket openings. Movies made her cry. Church made her cry. Dad made her cry. I decided I would never be like that. And I wasn't.

I've read that military brats don't attach. We make friends, but then somebody's dad gets a transfer, and we have to move. We learn to keep our relationships shallow. It's a well-researched phenomenon. But was it something in me that God wanted to fix? Was it healthy to cry about leaving home, or was that only appropriate for those left behind?

Life goes on, and you can't always figure yourself out. Maybe too much figuring is just another way of being self-centered. But today, as I left Michael at college, I thought of my mother watching the Volvo vanish around the corner. Michael was swept up in college fervor, eager to start his new adventure. He was so happy. How could I spoil it for him with tears? But now, in the car on the way home, I was crying like a baby. And I wished I could call Mom and tell her about it, say I was sorry I made her cry. Maybe I could attach, after all. Maybe there was still hope for me.

MY BRILLIANT IDEA

*M*om complained to Claire. The eggs were runny, there was no toast, everything was always the same. She pressed the call button and no one came. Was it Mom, or was it Azure Skies? In spite of its stellar reputation, online boasts, and premium rates, this arrangement was not working for us. I had hoped after we put Mom into this fancy-dancy establishment, my sister could begin to have a life again. And yet, she still must visit daily. Were we too picky? Was Mom too weird? Was Azure Skies just not that great? All of the above?

Now I was rethinking this whole deal. And I got an idea.

I began to pray about all of us --Claire and Arthur and Joel and me-- living in one house and taking care of Mom together.

One day in church, as I prayed and pondered, I felt God whispering, "Will you do this for Me?" The inaudible words hung in the air just above my head and slightly to the right, pulsing faintly like an invisible neon sign. It wasn't a demand or a test. He was just asking: Was I willing to get my body out to California and take care of Mom myself?

I didn't often hear from God so clearly. I was intrigued by His gentleness. It was like an invitation. *You come, too.*

Okay, I told God, *I'm willing to be willing. If I'm hearing You correctly, then I'll take it as confirmation if Deborah and Michael volunteer, without me asking them, that they're okay with me moving to California. And I'm not saying anything to Claire about all of us living together. If she gets this idea herself, I'll know it's from You.*

JUST HOLD HER HAND

*A*s I awaited clarity, I felt I should not take on any new ministries. I led a Bible study for college students from China. If I went to California, who would teach them?

~

THE WOMEN at my church would need some leaders to take my place if I left, so I offered a Bible study series for those interested in leadership development. If it turned out I mis-heard God, they would still profit from the experience.

I decided to take time off from coursework and resume studies in February 2014.

Meanwhile, calls and messages from Claire got more plaintive. She needed to vent. Mom kept asking, "What's it going to take to get me out of here?"

My sister was trying hard to make the best of things, but the cheerfulness she doggedly brought to Azure Skies was shot all to pieces within minutes of her arrival.

I wondered if I had any right to say this, because I wasn't the one doing the work. But I took a deep breath and told Claire, "I think you should change your goals from getting her to eat and drink, to touching her and making her laugh. Every time you visit, it's the same thing: she complains, you give her advice and encouragement. She ignores your advice and refuses to be encouraged. You feel hurt and angry. She feels your hurt and anger, and it makes her uncomfortable. Maybe what she really needs is for you just to hold her hand. Forgive her and love her as she is, for Jesus's sake, even if she doesn't appreciate anything. If you do that, when she goes you'll have peace."

My sister needed time to think about this. Claire had so many things to think about those days. She and Arthur had recently turned down a lowball offer on their Tennessee cabin. She was worried about money, and wondered what to do. The market was fine and the price was reasonable. Why was this taking so long?

A HAPPIER PLACE

With Michael in college, and no coursework for me till February, I was free to visit Mom. When Claire picked me up at the airport she informed me that the doctor had prescribed methadone.

"Methadone?" I exclaimed, raising my eyebrows. "Isn't that what they give you when you're trying to get off heroin?" Apparently, it has multiple applications.

Claire said, "Also, the activity director at Azure Skies sent around a memo inviting families to create memory portfolios for the residents. Do you have any ideas of things we could put in a portfolio for Mom?"

"Like what?'

"Oh, photos, I guess. Pressed flowers or fabrics, maybe. I don't really know."

"What's the point of a memory portfolio?" I asked.

"She wrote that if the resident is agitated or upset, we can use it to redirect them to a happier place."

Well, maybe. Till we could get that set up, there would be my smiling face to cheer Mom. When I arrived, she asked for ice cream. Why not? I pressed her call button.

We waited a long time, and no one came. Finally, I told Mom, "I'll go to the kitchen and get it myself."

On the way to the kitchen, I went to the front desk and asked if they had heard Mom's call button. No, said the receptionist. I asked to speak with the person in charge of communication. She would send him to Mom's room when he was available.

Mom was just finishing up her ice cream when Nick arrived, a sturdy-looking man in his forties. In my very best daughter-of-a-Texan-who-can-kill-with-politeness manner, I expressed my concern. "My mom is not very sure on her feet," I explained sweetly. "I need to know that someone will come when she rings the bell. What can we do about this?"

Nick promised he would get it working.

If they fix this call button problem, I thought darkly, *that will redirect me to a happier place.*

EPIC FAIL

*A*fter I returned to New Jersey. Claire sent an update:

When I visited Mom, she said she asked for milk, but no one had brought it. So I pressed her button, and no one came. I called the front desk and told them her button wasn't working, and the receptionist said she would leave a message for Nick. That has happened many times. I'm sending a request to Frank to replace the button entirely.

I thought, *Azure Skies, this is your one job.*

At the doctor's recommendation, Claire signed Mom up for hospice care. We were continually confronted with decisions. Should Mom get a feeding tube? A flu shot? What about her desire to be visited every day?

When Claire visited Mom, the urine odor made her stomach lurch. As she emptied the potty by the bed, she fumed, *Why should I have to do this? I'm here to visit, not clean up.*

She greeted Mom and pressed the call button. She pulled a chair close to the bed, sat down, and chatted amiably, taking care to make no remarks about food. Thirty minutes later, no one had responded. Claire was desperate. She had spoken, called and written to five people at Azure Skies, and been assured repeatedly that the problem would be solved.

There was one thing for Claire to feel happy about, however. After eleven months on the market, the cabin had sold. It would be one less thing to take care of, and it would bring Claire and Arthur a chunk of cash to invest else-where. Arthur was thinking Texas real estate.

CONFIRMATION

OCTOBER 2013
NEW JERSEY

*I*n October, Michael came home for Fall Break. Deborah and I were eager to see him. We laughed and ate and talked and drove all over New Jersey, visiting friends and running errands. I was glad I couldn't afford to put him on my auto policy, because I got to drive him everywhere. It was like old times. After Michael told us about his first weeks at college, and Deborah updated him on her life, I related Claire's emails and my recent interactions with Mom.

Michael observed, "Mom, West Orange isn't really my home."

"What do you mean?"

"Well," he said carefully, "the house in Bloomfield was always home. But after the divorce, when you and Dad sold the house, I didn't really think of anywhere as home any more."

I didn't either, really.

"If any place feels like home for me, it's the Oberlanders," he continued.

Paul and Connie's. Of course.

Then Michael added, "You don't have to stay here for me, Mom."

Deborah nodded, "Not for me, either. I mean, I love living with you and would like it better if you stayed here. But if you need to go to California to take care of Grandma, that's okay with me. Heck, maybe I'll even go with you."

Hmmm, I thought. *That's about as clear as it gets.*

Back at the West Orange apartment, my mind was awhirl. Deborah and I could move to Vista and have Mom live with us. If we had a part time caregiver, we could run errands and have time to ourselves. We could hire Cassidy, Arthur's niece, who has a CNA license.

Where would Michael go for holidays and summers?

What about my schooling?

How could I afford to live in California? Was my alimony sufficient?

I would clean the house, give Mom her meds, and feed her. Deborah could cook, hang with Mom, and do laundry.

Claire could continue to track Mom's medical needs and handle her finances.

I felt like I was right on the edge of Something Big, like I was feeling my way around for that last number, and a final twist to make all the tumblers click into place.

In one sense, the questions were moot. If God calls you to do something, you do it.

And yet, you have to ask, *How?* Practically speaking, *What do I do?*

CLAIRE'S BRILLIANT IDEA

NOVEMBER 2013
VISTA, CALIFORNIA

I was now on my fourth trip to California in a single year. As usual, Claire and I were enjoying a morning walk amongst the eucalyptus and pepper trees. We rambled uphill and down in shorts and tees, protected from UV rays by sunscreen, visors and dark glasses, on Vista's winding back roads, talking, always talking.

Also as usual, the topic of conversation was Mom.

"If there were some way for me to take more responsibility for her finances," I suggested, "that would be good. I'm good at that. You're better at the medical stuff."

"But explaining everything to you would be too much trouble. Mom's money situation is so complicated, and I'm still learning things myself."

"Well, I'm not crazy about the idea of hands-on care," I sighed. "But it makes sense for me to get a place here and just take care of her myself. With Deborah, and hired help, and you close by, it shouldn't be too bad. And we have hospice. Now that Michael's in college, there's no reason I couldn't do that. You've shouldered the lion's share of Mom's care long enough."

Claire shook her head. "If only we could think of some way to take care of Mom without you having to uproot yourself and come all the way here..."

"If I'm going to help as much as I should, I have to bring my body here. It won't be forever," I said.

"I have to admit you're right --if only there were some way for us to share equally in Mom's care. Some way that we would know she's okay, but neither of us would be excessively burdened."

Claire stopped walking, looked me straight in the eye, and said, "Wait, I have an idea. What if… what if…. we all move in *together* and take care of Mom? You and me, and Arthur and Joel? Maybe Deborah too?" She was thinking out loud now. "Of course, Arthur has his job, so he couldn't really help that much, but between you and me and the hospice people, and some hired help, we should be able to do it."

"What a brilliant idea," I beamed.

I could see Claire running calculations in her head. "If we sell our house, and combine that money with the proceeds from the Tennessee house, and Mom kicks in some, we could afford it, too. And Mom's income could pay for caregivers."

"Isn't Arthur in Texas this very minute, looking for investment properties?"

"Oh, right," she said. "I'll call him as soon as we get back and float the idea. He has to be on board. If he thinks it's a good idea, we should go for it."

My mother had an expression: "That was as easy as falling off a log backwards." For all my conjecturing, wondering and praying, I didn't have to convince anybody to do anything. My ideas were coming together by themselves, like dry bones rising up from the dirt and assembling themselves into skeletons. All I needed now was for God to add flesh and breathe life into them.

CRAFTING A PLAN

A few days later, Claire and I picked up Arthur at the airport. Usually, this was a task she did by herself, so they could talk on the drive home. Tonight was different. We were intent upon crafting a plan, the three of us.

Arthur was hungry, and the northbound 5 was a beast this time of day. We stopped at Milton's Deli, where a sign near the cash register read, "Keep Calm and Eat More Challah." When we were properly seated, Arthur ordered the chicken with vegetables, then pulled out his legal pad and announced, "I've been doing some calculations."

When Claire called, Arthur abandoned the idea of buying investment property and used his remaining time in Texas to think, research and plan. He laid his yellow legal pad on the table amidst the cutlery and glassware and showed us several pages of figures.

"You've really been thinking about this, haven't you?" I remarked.

Arthur leaned back in the padded booth and folded his hands on the table. "Well, I've been hearing Claire complaining about Azure Skies for --what is it?-- six months? Your mother is paying seven grand a month and what is she getting? She has an apartment, and people to give her medicine. They keep her from wandering off. But what else do they do?"

"They bring her food," I said.

Claire rolled her eyes. "Which she ignores."

Arthur continued, "They don't respond to her when she uses the call button. Frankly, their lack of responsiveness is not just annoying. It's dangerous."

He was right. Mom was paying for the paneled walls, the well-kept grounds, the cloth napkins. But what was she actually getting?

Arthur continued, "Claire has said that your mother's needs are somewhat unique. I mean, what she wants is not really in sync with what --to put it bluntly-- *normal* people want."

I nodded. The literature on Alzheimer's patients indicates they do much better with human contact. But Mom avoided anyone unfamiliar.

Arthur went on, "I agree with you and Claire that the extended-family-under-one-roof plan would make your mother happier and safer. If you're serious about this, we can get a four-bedroom house in this area and bring her home before the end of the year."

"Why so soon?" I asked.

"My business is quiet right now. The season picks up in January, but I'm relatively free till Christmas."

This was happening quickly. And yet I had known it was coming. Right now it felt like the most natural thing in the world to pack up and move across the country.

When we got back to Claire and Arthur's that night, I started making calls. Michael was positive. He and Deborah weren't really surprised. My older son Benjamin and his wife Corrie, who had seen her parents through multiple serious illnesses, voiced their support. Rebekah exclaimed "Wow. Wow." Even my ex-husband Ralph remarked sympathetically, "If you have to take care of your mom, you have to take care of your mom."

When I asked the hospice nurse for her opinion, she said Mom would be better off at home. She couldn't tell me if Claire and I would be better off at home with Mom. Nobody knew the answer to that question, except God. And He seemed to have already spoken.

WHERE SHALL WE LIVE?

Our real estate agent took us house-hunting. Claire, Arthur and I climbed out of the car, then stood on the wilted grass and stared. The house looked okay on one side, but the other side had an addition, a grotesque plaster appendix. Tramping through the rest of the building, we saw unfinished walls framed out, indicating where rooms were meant to be. Somebody started this project and didn't finish it. I couldn't imagine what they were trying to accomplish. And then we entered the older section of the house.

"Dear Lord," I exclaimed. "What is that extraordinary odor?"

"Pets," sighed Arthur.

"A *lot* of pets," I amended. "Incontinent pets, apparently."

This was the first in a series of disastrous houses. Later, we would refer to this dwelling as "the Peepee House."

Our agent showed us the Peepee House, the House with the Tiny Pointless Room, and the Rabbit Warren. The Rabbit Warren had six bedrooms, two kitchens, and no center. A perfect home for Flopsy, Mopsy, Cottontail and Peter, but not for us. I never guessed there were so many optimistically-commenced renovations gone hideously awry. Or that some people kept animals given to urinating so promiscuously that the house could only be sold as a demolition project.

THAT NIGHT I called my landlady and explained the situation. Would she allow me to break my lease without penalty? She had recently lost her own father. She said yes.

At the end of my visit, Claire and Arthur and I still hadn't found an appropriate dwelling for our blended family. San Diego County was unbelievably expensive. Maybe our calculations were too optimistic. Did we have enough money for this project?

I RETURNED to New Jersey to wrap up my commitments and begin packing. I'd just have to trust Claire and Arthur to find the right house. We were planning a January move-in, two months away. I was starting to feel a little scared. I needed to be sure about this.

I said to God, *"You know I don't usually play Bible roulette, but could You confirm Your will here?"*

I opened my Chronological Bible at random, and staring up at me was Deuteronomy 5:16.

> *Honor your father and your mother, as the LORD*
> *your God has commanded you, so that you*
> *may live long, and that it may go well with*
> *you in the land the LORD your God is*
> *giving you.*

Okay then.

THE AMAZINGLY LARGE HOUSE

*A*stonishingly, less than a week after Claire and Arthur's little house was listed for sale, they fielded six respectable offers. Compared to the difficulties of selling the Tennessee cabin, this was a walk in the park.

The timing of the sale of the cabin, and of the sale of the Prospect Place house, was perfect. Now we could leave behind rabbit warrens and urine-soaked kennels. Now that we had more cash to work with, the possibilities had expanded dramatically.

～

IN MID-NOVEMBER, Arthur and Claire found a promising ranch-style home with a nice view and a rambling back porch. I liked the orange trees on the property, and the wood floors inside.

When my sister went to Azure Skies to share the good

news, Mom didn't recognize her at first and began to cry when she realized her mistake.

Just a little while, Mom, and we'll bring you home. And you'll see us every day. I promise.

∼

AS THE MOVE DREW NEAR, I arranged to have my things shipped in containers. I could relocate while Michael was on Winter Break, so he and Deborah and I could drive my car across the US. We could see some new things, have fun experiences, and bond. He'd fly back to Pennsylvania from San Diego. I was practically rubbing my hands together with glee at the prospect of sharing a bucket-list cross-country trip with my two youngest.

FALLING INTO PLACE

DECEMBER 2013

*I*n early December, I called Mom for a chat. "Hey, It's Susan. How're you doing?"

"Oh, hello, you sweet thing! I was just lying here, waiting for something to happen. What's up with you?"

I talked about the children, the weather, the Bible studies. After a pause, she said, "I wish you could come out here and live close to me."

"Okay. Why not?" I said, as if she had suggested we go for ice cream. We laughed. Little did she know.

And did I mention that I was ridiculously happy to be planning the cross-country route?

BEFORE CLAIRE HAD her Brilliant Idea, I had made plans to spend Christmas with her and Arthur. This time my children and grandchildren joined us. We spent one last Christmas packed together in Claire and Arthur's house, where Rebekah and Josh announced, to everybody's joy, that she was pregnant. We visited the Amazingly Large House which was now ours, and everyone marveled at the size of the rooms and the back porch that went on forever. We fanned out over the property pulling blood oranges off the trees and eating them, juice dribbling luxuriously down our chins and onto our shirts.

Deborah decided to stay in New Jersey with a family from her church. After the California Christmas, we transferred her things to their house, and I packed my stuff into two elevator-sized cubes. The Big Move loomed, but I was prepared and everything was falling into place.

THE FALL

JANUARY 2014

*T*o my amazement, God provided a new Bible teacher for the Chinese students. The ministry team met one night to strategize and pray. At our hostess's home, we took off our shoes, muted our phones, and settled in. We drank many cups of tea and hammered out a plan. Everyone was satisfied.

On my way to the car, I fielded a call from Claire. "Hey," I answered. "What's up?"

"Where have you been? Why did you not answer my calls?"

"I was in a meeting. What's up?" I asked again.

"I'm at the hospital. Mom fell and hit her head."

The wintry air was whipping up my hair and smacking it against my mouth as I stood by the car. I couldn't think of how to get in. I felt disembodied. My sister's voice was all there was. "How serious is it?" I asked.

"Well, they say she has a cervical vertebra injury, and possible bleeding in the brain. That's the main thing. She has a big goose egg over her eye, and some cuts. Her wrist doesn't look that great, either. But the main thing is her brain."

Her brain. Three pounds of grey matter that control everything.

Somehow I got home. Home? My apartment was empty, soon to be occupied by a new tenant. In two days, I and my possessions were set to take two separate routes to California.

What was God up to? If Mom died now, why did I disrupt my entire life? If she lived through this, what would it be like taking care of her? Maybe she'd recover and be the same as before. It wasn't like her brain was in any great shape to begin with. Her neck bones weren't actually broken, just fractured. Maybe this was just a bump in the road.

Bump or not, my plan needed rejiggering. I booked a flight to San Diego and asked Connie and Paul if I could leave my car with them. They volunteered to finish cleaning my apartment, and to keep Michael until he went back to college.

Oh, I could've kissed them.

CHAOS

*A*rthur and Claire had spent the entire day moving furniture and boxes when Azure Skies called to tell them about Mom's fall. Naturally, they dropped everything and rushed to the hospital. While Claire filled out forms and talked with doctor after doctor, Arthur insisted on sitting by Ginny's bedside as she drifted in and out of consciousness. When Ginny was stable and there was nothing more to be done, he sent his wife home to rest. He'd get sleep when she returned in the morning.

Arthur sized up the situation as he hovered over his heavily-sedated mother-in-law. Dried blood was visible under the bandage on her swollen eyebrow. A cervical collar pushed her grizzled hair to the top of the pillow. Her bony arms were, as usual, covered with bruises, purple, green and yellow, some new and some old.

Arthur was dozing in a chair when he heard her stirring. Ginny was saying something. He hurried over and leaned in to hear. She murmured, "So this is the kitchen, huh?"

≈

I FLEW TO CALIFORNIA, weeping frustrated tears and wondering if God was really writing my story, or if I was just kidding myself.

You can't cry forever. By the time Joel picked me up at the airport, I was my usual composed self. We drove in the old rattletrap van to the Amazingly Large House which was now, appearances notwithstanding, my home. Claire and Arthur were at the hospital with Mom.

≈

BOXES HAD BEEN PILED ANYWHERE, higgledy-piggledy. Even on their best days, Claire and Arthur were not the most organized couple. I opened an unlabeled produce box and discovered a jumble of spiral notebooks and tea towels, three coffee cups and an extension cord. Further explorations revealed similarly random groupings of disparate household goods. Joel and I assembled a bed in my room and poked doggedly through bags and boxes until we found sheets, blankets, pillows. Lying in my cobbled-together bed, I stared out the curtainless windows into the night, wondering what was happening at the hospital a few miles away. The doctors told Claire that Mom's first vertebra might shift, which could result in a pinched spinal cord. I'm no expert, but a spinal cord seems like something that should not be pinched.

∼

THE FOLLOWING MORNING, I went to the hospital to sit with Mom while Claire and Arthur finished moving. The doctors and nurses came and went, and Mom slept.

One doctor said he thought Mom would recover. The hospice people, however, knitted up their eyebrows, bent their heads to one side, and pursed their lips in the classic expression adopted by medical personnel delivering a difficult diagnosis. "Mmmmm," they nodded sympathetically. They said Mom was shutting down and we should prepare for her imminent demise.

The next day, she looked better. She woke from time to time and talked nonsense, but seemed otherwise functional. I didn't believe she was shutting down.

Claire and Arthur and I took turns sitting with Mom, who slept deeply. From time to time her eyes would fly open and she would try to get out of bed, arms flailing. We couldn't leave her untended, and the nurses were too busy to keep an eye on her constantly. Later that week, when all three of us were loopy with fatigue, we hired someone from an agency to stay with Mom for twelve hours so we could all sleep.

∼

THE NEW HOUSE was still a chaotic landscape, boxes and bags strewn about, most now half unpacked, pawed through, and yawning open. Kelly, Claire and Arthur's black lab, sniffed quizzically at the mess and slept near the front door, and Sawyer, the cat, hid under the beds. No one could find anything, and all my stuff was still parked in New Jersey. That week, two toilets overflowed. We somehow got a plunger. There was no food. We all needed sleep. We wrestled our way to a temporary normal.

NEW NORMAL

Slowly, Mom pulled out of it. And slowly, we pulled things together in our new home. When a friend asked me to describe the house, I told her to type the address into realtor.com. "Holy crap!" she exclaimed, clapping her hand over her mouth. Our 3,300 square foot home rambled over half an acre of landscaping. The dog loved it. Directly outside my bedroom window was an orange tree heavily-laden with fruit. The soaring ceilings, granite countertops and stone mosaic tile were worlds away from the pink carpeting and dark wood window frames in the West Orange apartment.

It was to this home the medical transport brought Mom. She arrived on a gurney, laden with blankets, her neck held rigid in a stiff plastic brace. As the men pulled the gurney from the van, her wide eyes fixed on Claire, then Arthur, then me. She seemed to be awaiting an explanation. There was an awkward silence, as if she were a monarch newly-arrived on a royal palanquin, poised to deliver a stiff little speech. But of course, no speech was forthcoming. We threw open the big wooden doors and rolled her into the house. There was a brief kerfuffle as we all made suggestions for negotiating the turn in the hallway, and then there we were in Mom's new room.

The hospice had sent a wheelchair and an adjustable bed with rails on both sides. The room had thick carpeting, and a large window looking out on a Coast Live Oak. I found a plastic folding table amongst Claire and Arthur's things and commandeered it for books and a lamp. We installed the red arm chairs on either side of the bed and put the TV on top of a tall, narrow chest of drawers.

Well, she was all ours now.

Mom was unable to get out of bed or feed herself. But she was awake most of the time, trying to figure out what happened and where she was. She knew she didn't like the collar.

We needed someone in Mom's room constantly. When she wasn't sleeping, she tried to get out of bed, take off the collar, and pull out the catheter. We couldn't keep paying someone to sit up with her nightly. I found a twin mattress, dragged it into her room and decided to sleep there every night for the duration.

IN SPITE OF DIRE PREDICTIONS, Mom seemed likely to be with us longer than a few weeks. We decided to look into hiring a part-time caregiver. Claire and I met Cassidy, Arthur's niece with a CNA license, in our local coffee shop.

We chatted a while, nursing our drinks and watching customers come and go. When all the right questions had been asked and answered, we hired Cassidy to care for Mom four days a week, and breathed a sigh of relief.

A caregiver was wonderful during the day. But nights I was on my own.

I WAS LYING, dazed, on my mattress on the floor of Mom's room. She'd been awake since 3:00am trying to get out of bed. She rattled the rails with surprising energy and tugged at the irksome cervical collar. Her fingers sought a purchase on the Velcro straps holding it in place. I jumped up, feeling for her hands in the half-light. I guided them away from the collar and spoke soothingly. She glared at me and said, as if casting the blackest of aspersions, "You sure are interested in my cigs."

I dropped back onto the mattress. After a few moments of silence, as my mind relaxed into a sweet haze of slumber, I heard her once again working at the velcro. I leapt up and demanded, "What are you doing?" I explained that she must not remove the collar. She was astonished. I explained again and again. Again and again she lay impassively for a brief interval and then tried to remove the collar. I told myself I mustn't be angry with her for not remembering. "I need to pee," she pleaded. "Help me get to the bathroom so I can pee." She was confounded, again and again, to find this was also not permitted. All night long she was repeatedly bewildered, and I was exhausted.

What did Valerie say about learning her language? I couldn't remember.

I WAS FREQUENTLY grateful for Cassidy. Her presence allowed Claire and me to enjoy chunks of time to ourselves. My sister and I shared the newspaper, she reading it at breakfast, and I at lunch. Sections of the Wall Street Journal migrated from the breakfast table to the couch to my bedroom to the recycling bin. We kept seeing photos of Chinese mogul Jack Ma, which unaccountably amused us both. He was a glimpse of the outside world, a face that kept popping up like Kilroy.

Cassidy was a blessing, but she couldn't be there all the time. After trying a number of caregivers from the agency, we put in a standing order for Nifo, a sturdy Samoan woman with a no-nonsense manner.

LIVING WITH ALZHEIMER'S

y Matrix was still sitting in the Oberlanders' cramped driveway, buried in snow and waiting to be shipped to California. Meanwhile, I could take Claire's little car to the nearest beach at least once every weekend. The sand under my feet, the breeze, even the cold water were just like they were forty years ago. Forty years from now, when I was gone, the waves would still spread hurriedly up the beach and slide back in the same eternal systole and diastole.

I developed a routine. I parked at the northern end of town, away from the touristed area, took the narrow, palm-lined stairs down to the water, and headed south, toward the jetty. Usually there were tourists throwing frisbees, making sandcastles, body surfing. It was hard to think dark thoughts when I saw a couple walking hand in hand, or snuggling under a blanket, or playing with a baby.

I chugged along on the wet sand till I arrived at the jetty, reaching out to tag one of its boulders, then turned around and trudged north, the sun on my left shoulder. On the way back there was a coffee shop which sold excellent iced decaf. By the time I reached the car and finished buffing the sand off my bare feet, I felt almost human again.

One day I decided to stop at KFC on the way home. When we lived in Lake Forest, Mom used to take us to KFC after church on Sunday, and buy whatever we wanted for lunch, which for me was always a juicy fried chicken breast and a buttery biscuit. Mom would ask for a "center breast, crispy." Nowadays, a piece of fried chicken would meet a tragic end in Mom's hands. I could just imagine the greasy carnage. But I could still get her some crispy strips and a good old biscuit.

I returned home before lunchtime, bearing chicken, and arranged the treats fetchingly on a tray: Southern sweet tea, chicken strips, a biscuit with honey, fresh strawberries, and a piece of dark chocolate.

"Hey, Mom," I called, as I entered her room. "I brought fried chicken."

She didn't exactly crow with delight. But she did eat some of it, including all the chocolate. It was the best I could hope for these days: convincing Mom to ingest calories, any calories.

My father's illness made me think differently about food. As he lay dying, I tried to think of something I could make for him to tell him I loved him without actually uttering the unforgivably sentimental words "I love you." He offhandedly expressed a wish for a bread pudding such as his mother used to make. I hunted up the recipe in Mom's old Betty Crocker cookbook, and discovered -- merciful heavens!-- bread pudding was chockablock with unhealthy ingredients: whole eggs, heavy cream, white bread, white sugar. I shut the cookbook in disgust. But then I reconsidered. He already had cancer. What could bread pudding do to him now but just make him happy?

I made the pudding, and he enjoyed it.

Dad's illness progressed on schedule, as if he read the hospice pamphlet and methodically checked off the boxes: denial; loss of appetite; loss of bladder and bowel control; withdrawal; restlessness; agitation; the final, awful burst of energy when he tried to get out of bed; all the way to the coma and death rattle. It was horrifying, but we knew what to expect, and when to expect it.

The inexorable progress of Dad's disease was scary, but dementia was different. If Dad's journey was a well-mapped path, Mom's was Mr. Toad's wild ride. What would happen? When? In what order? Nobody could tell us. Arthur said that in the end, Alzheimer's patients lose the ability to swallow. The hospice nurse told us bedridden patients often die from infections. In Mom's case, urinary tract infections were a constant threat because of the catheter. But if we removed the catheter, frequent expo-sure to urine would invite bedsores. I asked Rachel, "How bad are bedsores, anyway?"

"Oh, they're terrible. I treated one last week that was

down to the bone," she responded cheerfully. "You want to do everything you can to prevent them." So Mom kept the hated catheter, though she never fully made peace with it. Nor would I, in her position.

WITHERED CAULIFLOWER

FEBRUARY 2014
VISTA, CALIFORNIA

*D*uring the day, I tapped away at the computer, writing research papers. One evening when it was my turn to sit with Mom I curled up in one of the cushy chairs and read a textbook while she stared at a crossword puzzle book. Mom had always loathed boredom and kept a supply of novels and puzzle books of various types all around the house to occupy herself in idle moments. I had ordered this one for her when she lived at Omnia. Now it just sat on a table until someone handed it to Mom as a diversion. She would hold it, looking perplexed, until it finally slipped from her fingers, and one of us would quietly put it back in its place. Leafing through the book, I saw that as recently as two months before she was able to shakily scrawl in the answers. Toward the end of the book, larger and larger portions were left blank, and the writing was more cramped. Finally, the rest of the puzzles were completely empty.

I looked up Alzheimer's disease on the internet, and saw a cross-section of a human brain. It looked like cauliflower. On the left side of the picture, the cauliflower was plump and fulsome. Underneath was the caption, "Healthy brain." On the right side was another piece of cauliflower, shrunken and wilted. The caption underneath read, "Severe Alzheimer's."

Sometimes my mother was sweet and grateful, and she held my hand and we laughed. I asked God to give me compassion and tenderness with her, and He was changing my heart. I tried to consider the way she perceived things now, with her wizened cauliflower brain. She used to be so on top of things, and now she was so .... *not*. How well would I do as an Alzheimer's patient? My compassion was tinged with fear. I wanted to put myself in Mom's shoes so I could have empathy for her. But those shoes were so scary that I recoiled each time I came near them. I was haunted by withered cauliflower.

VISTA, CALIFORNIA/CHERRY POINT, NORTH CAROLINA

FEBRUARY 2014/AUGUST 1959

*I*n February, Benjamin, my oldest, announced that he had accepted a professorship in Lithuania. He, his wife, and two small children would fly there from Philadelphia in August. I found Lithuania on a map and prayed for them, wondering, *How can I let them go?*

ONE DAY MOM beckoned Claire with a clawlike hand and whispered hoarsely, "I need to speak with you privately." Claire sent Cassidy to the kitchen for fresh water, then asked, "What's the matter?"

"I have it all planned out," Ginny began.

What is 'it'? wondered Claire. Mom continued talking as if she thought she were making sense, but none of her words hung together in cogent sentences. Claire listened, nodding, then extricated herself for a much-needed walk when Cassidy returned.

Good old Claire. I was glad she had Cassidy and Nifo to help her, Arthur for moral support, a cat to cuddle, and the beautiful San Diego sunshine to enjoy.

Good Old Claire. I almost lost her. Twice.

IN THE FALL OF 1959, First Lieutenant Keith Soesbe squatted beside his car, checking the tire pressure. His young wife Ginny stood behind him, baby Claire in her arms, talking about their upcoming road trip. Keith had received orders to report to Camp Pendleton, and they had less than a week to move from Camp Lejeune in North Carolina to another military base in Southern California. As he bent to unscrew the cap from the gauge stem, he felt a sudden, wet slap on his back, as if someone had flung a freshly-cooked pancake between his shoulder blades. He turned to see baby Claire, not yet six weeks old, drooling the last curd-clotted dregs of her breakfast onto her cotton smock.

"Dag nabbit! What was that? Does she always do that?" he exclaimed.

Ginny nodded. "It's normal for babies to spit up sometimes."

"I don't think that's normal. Has she been to the clinic?"

"I took her last week. The doctor said she's fine."

Keith appraised his daughter, who regarded him impassively. Her belly was round enough, but her arms and legs were thin, her eyes dull. "When we get to California, I think you should take her to the clinic on base."

Ginny sighed. "All right. It couldn't hurt, could it?"

At the Camp Pendleton clinic, the doctor gaped at my sister. "Have you been feeding this baby?" he demanded.

"I do almost nothing else," Ginny retorted. "I started nursing her, but then she was spitting up so much the doctor in Camp Lejeune put her on formula. She kept throwing that up too, so I tried a different formula. She eats all the time. It's just that she spits it all up." As Ginny spoke, a flume of half-digested formula erupted from Claire's mouth, shot across the room and hit the wall with a soggy splat.

The doctor said, "I think I know what's wrong."

In the weeks after her birth, the aperture between Claire's stomach and small intestine had thickened, leaving almost no opening through which fluid could pass. Again and again, the milk she frantically drank, finding no egress, was ejected forcefully in one convulsive spasm. Claire was starving, dehydrated, and on the verge of death. An accurate diagnosis and a simple surgery saved her life. What if Dad hadn't gotten those orders to report to Camp Pendleton? What if someone at the clinic there hadn't figured out what was wrong or didn't know what to do about it? What would my life be like without Claire?

She played school with me, got me to do skits and dance routines, walked me to school. We rode bikes, pushed each other on the swings, played Barbies together.

We borrowed each other's books, magazines and clothes. We fought, fumed and fussed. She taught me to drive.

When we were young adults, I took my path and she took hers. She wrote to me frequently, but I was too busy with church and children to respond much. One day a letter arrived telling me she felt hurt. "Each of us is the only sister that the other one has. If we don't make the effort to stay in touch, we will lose each other. I need to hear from you more often."

So I stepped it up. Claire had always been there for me. She knew me better than anyone. What if I had let her go?

GETTING IT DONE

MARCH 2014

*C*laire adopted a proprietary attitude toward Mom's urinary output and bowel movements, like a mother caring for an infant. She periodically pulled the briefs away from the skin to have a look, prompting Mom to exclaim with justifiable indignation, "What are you doing?"

Claire would say with unassailable candor, "I'm checking your drawers." It's funny what you can normalize if you just speak calmly without dissembling.

By now we had each adopted various roles. Claire was the checker of drawers and the wiper of privates. When we rolled Mom into a fresh position, I was the hefter of the underpad. Claire was the stuffer, folding pillows in half lengthwise and cramming them under the pad to prop Mom up.

Claire also served as the arranger of legs. She would

stand back and study the position of Mom's emaciated limbs, then place pillows between knees and under heels for maximum comfort and circulation.

I was the one who changed Mom's shirt and washed her face. Claire brushed her teeth.

Claire was the emptier of the catheter bag and the recorder of urine.

Claire ordered medicines and supplies, and I procured entertainment in the form of books, magazines, DVDs and various objects.

Claire scheduled and paid the caregivers, and I freshened the air, dusted, cleaned and straightened up.

I still sometimes wondered if I was doing enough. But between us, we got it done.

WORSHIP

*M*om woke early on a Sunday morning, and announced, "I need to go to the bathroom." I explained, yet again, about the fall, the concussion and the catheter. Again, she was uncomprehending. Sadly, I was still unskilled at redirecting my mother to a happier place.

Now she was picking at the blankets, pulling the case off a pillow and examining it closely as if to ascertain its purpose. She pulled the silky blue material through her thumb and forefinger like a cloth merchant.

Maybe a movie would calm her. I slid *A Christmas Carol* into the DVD player. When Scrooge had been thoroughly reformed and the credits were rolling, Mom was tranquil. I wanted to move on with my day: Bible reading, prayer, a walk, church, lunch. But I couldn't focus while she was awake. I thought, *Why not start church now?* I put on a worship CD, closed my eyes, and listened to the words.

On a hill far away stood an old rugged cross,
The emblem of suff'ring and shame;
And I love that old cross where the dearest
    and best
For a world of lost sinners was slain.

I'm a little girl, sitting beside my mother on a shiny wooden church bench. The congregants are worshipping in song, some bent over red hymnals, others with faces uplifted. Ginny chants tunelessly along, barely audible. Claire, sitting on the other side of my mother, is wearing the red plaid dress I covet and will someday grow into. Soon my sister and I will adjourn to a room with the other children, and a smiling lady wearing a floral dress and sensible shoes will tell us a story about Jesus and refresh us with vanilla sandwich cookies and sweet red juice.

I opened my mouth and sang along with all my heart. I knew most of the words. Mom was quiet in her hospital bed, as unmoving as if seated on a hard pew. Her hands were still.

LEARNING TO FORGET

A few days later, Mom and I have enjoyed *Despicable Me 2*, and she's watching me take the DVD out of the player and put it into its case.

"How many tapes are up there?" she asks. I dutifully count: thirteen DVDs.

"Name them for me," she demands. So I do.

She struggles to get out of bed. "What do you want?" I ask.

"I'm trying to get over there so I can see all those tapes," she says, as if this were obvious to anyone with even a single brain cell. I bring the stack of DVDs to her, and she minutely examines each case, holding each in turn up to her good eye. Again, she makes as if to get up and go somewhere.

"What are you doing?" I ask.

"Give me strength," she mutters, rolling her eyes at my

extreme idiocy. "I want to give this one back to the Russians."

"I can give it to the Russians," I offer.

"Are you sure? How?"

"I'll take it over there right now."

"You'll just go over there and take it to them?"

"Yes," I assure her.

"Okay," she responds, clearly skeptical. Fortunately, my sister enters the room. I walk out and stand in the hallway, leaning against the wall with my arms crossed and eyes closed. I'm sick of this who's-in-the-right oneupmanship. It's past time to let go of that. So I decide to forget this ever happened. I'm sure she's already forgotten.

A VISIT FROM THE HOSPICE NURSE

*L*ater that week, Rachel came for her weekly check of Mom's vitals. When she was finished, she sat down with me and Claire in our sunny living room to discuss her findings.

We spoke of Mom's new habit of using a pen to poke holes in her blanket. We voiced our hope that, since her fractured vertebra was healed, Mom would be able to get up and use the wheelchair to get around, use the potty chair on her own. Or maybe even just sit up from time to time.

"She would be a tremendous fall risk," explained Rachel. "With her muscle loss and poor coordination, she would end up falling, which would not be good."

Claire and I nodded. Mom couldn't afford another fall.

"I took her vitals, and it looks to me like her organs are beginning to shut down."

Claire and I exchanged a glance.

I responded for us both, "I find that hard to believe. I mean, she seems okay to me."

Rachel explained that Mom's forearm measurement had gone down by 2 cm; her pulse was high and her blood pressure very low. These were signs of organs shutting down.

Claire looked perplexed, and all I could say was "Oh."

Because when she was in the hospital, the hospice people said Mom was "shutting down." But she was still alive two months later.

It wasn't that I wanted her to hurry up and die. I just wanted to pace myself. I only had so much time, energy and attention to give. Should I splurge this week, since Mom has only days left? Or should I eke it out in reasonable servings over the course of weeks and months?

How could I give Mom what she needed and still keep up with my degree work? Keep up with other relationships? Exercise and do laundry? Where should I draw a line?

Every day the same question: *Where's the line, and how do I find it?*

Sawyer the cat leapt delicately onto the couch beside Rachel. She scratched his head and ran her hand along his back. Here we all sat, in the afternoon sunshine. It was so still and pleasant.

"Well, I'll see you next week. Call me if you need anything," said Rachel.

LOSING TOUCH

*W*ell, I didn't think Mom was shutting down. I'd heard *that* before. I couldn't put my life on hold forever. The following week, I decided to go on a whale-watching excursion with my old friend Julie.

Julie's mother had died recently after a long, difficult illness. We both could use a day in the fresh air and sunshine. As the boat pulled out of the harbor, I told Julie about my schedule, my difficulty sleeping, our worries about Mom's care. As the boat undulated on the waves, and people around us leaned over the handrails talking and laughing, Julie laid her hand on my arm and said quietly, "Maybe you should see a minister for counseling."

Was it that bad?

She said, "You sound like you're in need of some help."

It's hard to know when you need help and when you should just suck it up. Some things can't be helped. But why did I always have to stop my life and sit vigil? When I thought like this, I felt guilty.

Maybe I did need help. Mom was losing touch with the rest of the world, and now so was I.

A friend from New Jersey, who brought her husband's mother into her home for care, told me her mother-in-law confused television with real life.

Oh, come on, I thought. *That's bizarre. That will never happen to my mother.*

Two months in, that happened to my mother. One evening she beckoned me to the bed, pulled me close, and whispered, terrified, "The police are in the house, and they have guns." I briefly recalled reading something which referred to the increased agitation and confusion in dementia patients in the evening as "sundowning."

I told her the policeman was our friend, someone to protect us. When would I learn that logic is lost on a person with dementia? She said she wouldn't feel safe until they were gone. I'd become convinced of the compassion of white lies, so I assured her they'd left.

She'd been watching the old television show *Emergency!* I switched the channel to *Mayberry RFD*.

When I tried to find some soothing, happy videos, I quickly realized that even the mildest programs have some sort of suspense or peril. Even the lovely animated *The Tale of Peter Rabbit* is fraught with tension. Peter is pursued by the terrifying Mr. McGregor, whose wife, the story goes, has already put Peter's father into a pie.

Then I realized that old family videos would handily

answer my purpose. They had no plot, the performers were on their best behavior, and the kids were really cute. Perfect.

LIFE IS GOOD

So this was my life. I woke with the sunrise, glided past my still-sleeping mother, and made my way to the front door. I opened it and padded down the chilly, damp walkway in bare feet. The snails were always out early enjoying the sprinklers and the relative coolness: I'd have a foot full of slime if I didn't watch my step. The birds twittered and flitted in the orange trees and the sky was still, as if waiting. The bougainvillea shifted a bit in a faint breeze, its riotous magenta blossoms fluttering slightly. I reached into the stiff citrusy branches, picked an orange, peeled and ate it, staring at the ants scurrying up and down the tree trunk.

It was like this, with little variation, every day. I lived in Zone 23, a thermal belt of the coastal climate. Essentially a desert by the ocean.

I could drive to the beach in fifteen minutes. Even hit

Trader Joe's on the way and pick up a sprout salad for four dollars, kombucha for another three.

When my East Coast friends asked, "How is California?" they were asking me to tell them how I was doing in my new situation. Well, if the weather were the only factor, I would have said my life was swell. But weather is only one aspect of life.

I missed my friends. I had a great family, and they loved me. My sister and I still played, in our way, by taping up random pictures in random places. Once I found an advertisement for pest control in my side of the pantry which read, "Rats are *everywhere!*"

Then there was Mom, who kept pushing those old buttons. I told myself she didn't mean to, but it was hard not to clench up sometimes. God gave me do-overs, and I was slowly learning to let it go.

I took online classes in three-month chunks, chipping away at that Bachelor's degree. I worked on long-term projects, like trying to get the house organized.

God called me there, but I wasn't crazy about my work. It was exactly against my grain. I was impatient, direct, and creative. Now I was taking things slowly, answering Mom evasively, and doing the same things every day.

And every day I would remind myself that I wasn't the one who was dying. Well, at least not as quickly as Mom.

Life was good. Yes, life was good in California. Everywhere, really.

KEEPING THE PEACE

Ginny holds out her cupped hands and asks "How long do I have to hold on to these?"

"You don't have to hold on to those if you don't want to," Claire replies smoothly.

"Well, what am I supposed to do with them?"

"I can take them for you."

My mother extends her empty hands. Claire takes possession of the unwanted invisible items and puts them into her pockets.

Mom lies back, relieved. As if she had given my sister an apronful of live hand grenades.

We often had to wing it. Another time Mom beckoned me to her bedside. When I drew near, she whispered, through clenched teeth, "Get out of here!"

Taken aback, I asked, "Why?"

"They're going to *shoot* you," she hissed, in agony.

What could I do? I left. It later occurred to me that she

didn't care at all if Nifo, also in the room, were shot dead. Perhaps I shouldn't have been surprised, since she had recently called Nifo, to Claire's intense embarrassment, "that blob in the corner."

My college courses challenged me to think and write logically. But in this role I was forced to use a language of appeasement. There was no reasoning with Mom, only a sort of coming alongside and gently steering. At all costs, avoid the turbulence of argument, correction or offense. She had no tools for handling these, and it would be cruel to engage her on the customary terms.

RAMPING IT UP

APRIL 2014

*J*ulie and I went to high school together in the 1970s, when teenagers still drove around in cars and went out to movies. Julie and I explored Southern California in her white VW Beetle, having adventures and yukking it up. Thirty-five years later, here we were, perhaps less exuberant, but still having fun and talking, always talking.

Julie wasn't giving up on me yet. The memories of her own mother's protracted illness were painfully fresh. When I made those frequent trips from New Jersey to California, Julie would take me for lunch and long drives. We both needed to get away. She made a habit of listening, and now, more than ever, I needed to be heard.

Today, in the car with Julie, I shared my struggles again.

"I need to explain this," I told her, propping my bare foot on the dashboard. "For years I've been critical of my

SUSAN SOESBE

mother's life choices. She spent too much time watching soap operas, bowling, and playing bingo. She nagged at Dad, when she could have made his life very pleasant. She said she was a Christian and attended church every Sunday. But when we talked, I just felt like Jesus wasn't all that important or relevant to her. I honestly felt like I couldn't share the things I was learning and what God was doing in my life. She wouldn't get it."

"She wasn't on the same level as you, religiously?"

"I guess you could put it that way. Christians have a certain expectation that we're supposed to get more... spiritual, more.... holy... as we get older. It's not okay to just be the same person. That's why it's called 'being born again.' You start out as a spiritual baby, but you're supposed to grow. To keep repenting of sin as God shows you where you're going wrong. You're supposed to be letting God shape you into a person who's fit to live with Him forever," I explained, somewhat hesitantly. Julie was an atheist, and we seldom spoke of this subject. Frustration was making me reckless.

"So, you were critical of your mom, because she wasn't being a good Christian?" Julie ventured, taking her eyes off the road for an instant to glance my way.

I winced. "Well....yes. But here's how it affects me today. One of the hardest things for Claire and me is the fact that Mom has never properly cared for her body. She's always considered food as solely for pleasure. As long as I've known her, she's eaten mostly processed foods. You remember visiting when we were in high school. Mom never cooked. She bought. We ate canned soups, sandwiches, chips, ice cream."

"I remember," nodded Julie. "And you and Claire went in exactly the opposite direction. You guys are so healthy now."

"We grew up and discovered actual cooking," I laughed. "We liked it. We liked feeding our families real food."

"But you still love your mother. You take care of her. Everybody disagrees with people sometimes. Don't be too hard on yourself."

I knew Julie would say this. She loved me. It was hard to argue this point with her.

"Well, I do love her, but I judged her for bad food choices, and I felt resentful about it because in her final years of living alone her diet seemed almost entirely chocolate with an occasional BLT. I resented Mom letting herself get into such a state. And yet," I concluded, "Maybe her brain's been declining all this time, and her increasingly poor choices have been her way of coping. Maybe I should see her as a brave survivor who lived on her own as best she could, given her declining executive function."

"That sounds right," Julie agreed, making a smooth left onto another winding back road. She loved to explore. "Wouldn't that make it easier to take care of her?"

I nodded. "But it's so hard. I've hardened my heart towards Mom."

Julie was quick to excuse my lack of love. She pointed to my dedication and sacrifices, and reminded me I'm only human. She was kind. And she was right. The Biblical standard of love was too high for me. I needed the Spirit of

Christ to dwell in my heart. I needed Him to come and stay, to unpack His bags and set up shop. He alone could reveal ugly things in my heart and then remove them. But usually the things only come away piece by piece.

I was venting to Julie again because Alzheimer's was ramping it up. So I had to ramp it up.

Recently Mom had been demanding —not asking, demanding— that I get into bed with her. I was loath to do so. Though it would make her feel secure and warm and loved, something in me recoiled at the thought.

After Julie dropped me off, I settled in with Mom, curling up with my book in a chair by the bed. "I'm cold," she said. Except for pain, she seldom indicated awareness of her body, so I spread another blanket on the bed and turned up the space heater. A few minutes later, I asked, "Are you still cold?"

She said yes. I know how miserable it feels to be chilled. Something inside me slid away, like a heavy backpack. I lowered the rail and carefully climbed onto the edge of the bed, next to her fragile body, and cuddled her. We lay quietly that way for a long time. It was all right.

BETWEEN HEALTHY AND DEAD

*E*ach Sunday at church, the pastor invited attendees to come to the front to be prayed for. So today I shouldered my way through the crowd and approached a sympathetic-looking prayer volunteer. When I told her my mother had Alzheimer's, she said, "That's when you lose your memory, right?"

Well, yes and no. How could I explain that Mom didn't know what her toothbrush was?

Sometimes she couldn't even remember how to suck on a straw.

She would occasionally raise her hands above her head and hold them there for fifteen minutes or more, even while sleeping. Her fingers contracted into fists like those of a paralyzed person. I could no longer wedge a pill or a grape between her thumb and forefinger so she could convey it to her mouth. The only way to be sure all the medicine would go down was to crush it all up and mix it into chocolate ice cream.

She reached out for things that weren't there, and asked what they were.

Her abilities and her mood kept changing.

Today she was up at 5:00am. She threw off the blankets, tried to sit up, seized the bed rails and rattled them with all her might. By the time I calmed her down and she went back to sleep, I was fully awake.

But none of these things was the problem. The problem was me.

I said to the prayer lady, "I need Jesus to help me love my mom better." I told her there was a good cry under the surface, and I felt very tired and sometimes peevish. She took my hands in both of hers and prayed for me, fervently, from the heart. Her faith buoyed me up.

I LOVED HOSPICE CARE. The support we got, practically and emotionally, was incalculable. To continue receiving hospice benefits, my mother needed to get recertified every ninety days. When the time for recert drew near, I began to feel tense. What if Mom didn't qualify?

Shouldn't I have been hoping that Mom got well enough to not need hospice care any more? Shouldn't I have been praying for healing?

Does God heal? The Bible says He can, and does. Does He heal everyone? No. More to the point, should I have been praying for Mom to get well, or for her to just keep looking really sick?

I had already prayed for her to be healed of dementia. Should I have kept asking for this? What did I expect? The Bible doesn't teach that anyone, even one with perfect faith, will be healthy and never die. Instead, it depicts a world marred by sin and sickness, in which all are destined to die and eventually to rise again. But in the meantime, the Bible also tells us to pray for healing.

I didn't like this intermediate condition --between healthy and dead.

"Dear God," I whispered in my bed at night. "Please keep taking care of us all, however You manage to do it. If hospice goes away, You'll provide something. Help us honor our mom."

One thing I hadn't counted on: Mom's catheter often leaked, sometimes badly enough to soak an entire disposable brief. Today I watched closely as Cassidy rolled my mother onto her side, peeled off the diaper, and deftly wiped, wiped, wiped. She stuffed the urine-soaked brief under the wizened buttock and tucked a fresh brief right next to the old one, then turned Mom to the other side. She then reached under from the other side to finally pull away the old brief and position the fresh one correctly. She did this repeatedly throughout the day.

I was watching so I could do this on my own. Claire and Arthur would leave soon for a ten-day vacation. Claire and I had made this a two-person job, but I needed to make it a one-person job. If Cassidy could do it, so could I.

Every day at 5:30pm, the caregiver left. Mom usually slept then, so the rest of us ate in the kitchen, keeping an eye on her through a video monitor. Now we could enjoy a family dinner. Arthur would hold forth on a subject of mutual interest, usually bringing news that Claire and I had missed. We got a daily newspaper just to keep in touch with the outside world. And sometimes see pictures of Jack Ma, of course.

Nowadays I washed up and brushed my teeth at the ridiculous hour of 8:00pm. By 9:00, Mom usually dozed off and I read by the light of a bed lamp as long as I could.

After turning off the light, I lay there and wondered if I'd wake to find Mom dead. It wasn't an outlandish thought: hospice was for people who were dying. Mom was living, and she was dying. So was I. I got all philosophical lying alone in the dark. Sometimes Mom snored a little, and that made me feel better.

One day soon she would die. She would die while one of us was with her, or she'd die alone and one of us would find her. I kept steeling myself for this. I didn't want it to happen, but it would anyway. I dreaded that moment. And when it occurred, I'd be gobsmacked.

EASTER SUNDAY

*M*om woke up with gunk in the corners of her eyes. I said, "Good morning."

"Who is *he?*" she asked. Dementia may have robbed her of facial expression, but she made up for it with a scornful tone.

"Who is who?" I responded.

She glared. "The one you're talking about."

"I'm not talking about anyone. I said 'Good morning.'"

She was silent. Maybe thinking this over. No, probably not. I examined the catheter tube and played my usual game of feeding the urine over the loops until it was all drained into the bag hanging on the bed rail. Today the urine was a clear yellow, like lemonade. We'd recently made it through a urinary tract infection, which yielded dancing blooms of whitish sediment in rust-colored urine. So the tube of clear fluid, warm in my fingers, pleased me.

I felt I should hug her, but her breath was putrid. Claire

still tried to brush Mom's teeth nightly, but she couldn't outpace the bacteria.

When I was a child, I would get up, get dressed and *go*. I didn't think about my body till I was tired, thirsty, hurt or hungry. But now my gums are receding, my muscles are losing tone, my skin has gotten crepey.

We die a little every day, the sand sliding down continually in the hourglass until the last grain is deposited.

Tomorrow we would celebrate Easter. Jesus was the first person to be raised from the dead in a brand new body. His followers expect to be raised the same way, to live with Him forever on a brand new earth. I believed in science and in nature, because I could see the world around me. I also believed in a God who could do miracles if He liked.

It takes no faith at all to know that death will eventually catch up with you. It takes faith to believe you'll live on after you die, in a new kind of body, which is as much like your present body as a plant is like a seed.

I wondered, *Does the sown seed feel like it's dying or like it's just beginning to live?*

A LIFE WORTH LIVING

MAY 2014

*M*om seemed better lately. She lay in her bed, staring out the window at the exuberance of spring flowers. She wasn't agitated or frightened. We didn't talk, because she had nothing to say, and when I said things, she didn't get it. One day I entered her room and announced, "I brought you a Cinnabon!" And she responded, "a synagogue?" I chuckled intermittently for hours, then cried that night. Sometimes I wondered if I was okay.

So it occurred to me that she may be around for a while. Which was great. Right? Wasn't that the whole point?

The thing was, my kids and grandkids were three thousand miles away, and my son and his family would soon be moving to a Baltic state. I could go with them. Oh, wait, I had this commitment.

How could I guard against the clear and present danger of wishing Mom would die so I could get on with my life?

If she had a life I thought was worth living, I would have felt better about having rescued her from her chandeliered prison. I didn't regret moving here, but I had to wonder what I thought it was going to be like.

I remembered now. It was supposed to be like her life in Texas, only in California, with me and Claire and Arthur. I imagined her life would like one of those television commercials with wrinkled but smiling people hugging each other in slow motion, while Louis Armstrong warbles "What a Wonderful World." In my mind's eye, we talked, laughed, and enjoyed games. She did puzzles and watched TV. She would recline on a patio chaise, smell flowers and eat fresh oranges off the trees. My idea of Mom's life at home with us involved more interaction, more warmth and, well…. meaning.

But then she fell and fractured her neck, languished in bed for weeks, and couldn't walk any more. Dementia squatted in her head, a malevolent tangle of amyloid plaques, and now here she was, like this. I hadn't imagined this.

But God must think Mom's life was still worth living, or she would be gone. And if He thought I should be with my grandchildren, He would direct me there.

So I was asking God the question I always asked, which is "Why? Where's the meaning?"

I asked a friend who was a hospital chaplain. Her answer to life, the universe and everything always looped back to *pray and trust God*. Yeah, I knew that. But what about the *answers?*

I kept asking, and God responded like always, *Here I am.*

So it was just the old trust and obey thing, like the hymn. Easy to sing, hard to do. No, I didn't want Mom to die. I wanted her to live. I wanted all of us to live and be happy and have peace with God and each other. But we were in this in-between, now-and-not-yet world. And how did it all work, anyway? Trust was required. And I was learning it, I hoped, one Cinnabon at a time. Synagogue. Whatever.

PUSHING BUTTONS

*A*s they say, life goes on. I made plans to go to Illinois in late July for the birth of my daughter Rebekah's baby.

Meanwhile, Deborah announced that her New Jersey hosts planned to move. Could she live with us? She would have to move into the room where I did stuff when I wasn't sleeping or watching Mom. It would be hard to share my space, but I told her yes. I wanted to be more like the Oberlanders, who were more like Jesus. And Deborah was a very compassionate person. She could help with Mom. Maybe this was just the encouragement I needed to buck up my performance.

Claire and I had spent the last forty-five minutes getting Mom comfortable for the night. Claire made sure the cat hadn't snuck in, then turned out the light and closed the door behind her.

Now I was settled on my mattress, bent over a textbook. All was quiet, and I could cram a few more facts into my brain before drifting off.

I liked it better when Mom was turned to her right, where she couldn't see me. Tonight, whenever I snuck a look up at her bed, her sunken eyes were fixed on me. I felt stalked.

Suddenly she said, "Well, just let it *glare* in my eyeballs."

An old string shuddered up and down the length of my heart. "Do you mean to tell me that my reading light is bothering your eyes?" I asked in measured tones.

"Yes," she said in her best *you're-an-idiot* voice.

"Well, then, maybe you could couch that as a question rather than as a statement," I suggested frostily, turning back to my book.

I felt like she'd dragged up every offense from the past fifty-two years and thrown it over the bed rail onto my little mattress.

Mom had always been sarcastic. It was her primary mode of communication. For Ginny, it would never do to say something plainly. It must always be exclaimed about and deplored with indignation: "Of course your father had to buy the *most expensive* one," "The *one* day the mailman comes early is the day I needed him to wait so I could put this in the mail," "That *stupid* old dog woke me up by barking his head off," etc.

But there was more to it. She was always making a covert accusation. Why couldn't she say, instead, "Your light bothers me. Could you turn it so that it's not beaming straight into my eyes?"

It was even more than that. It was the implication that I

didn't care. That I was selfish. That there was nothing she could do but suffer nobly in silence, because I had knowingly, callously, willfully and with malice aforethought, allowed my light to shine directly into her eyes.

As long as I had known her, every disappointment was met with some variation of the lament, "No one cares about me."

My friend Cindy, who is patient and kind, and who loves her job working with elderly people, would say, "That's the disease talking." But it wasn't. That was exactly what Mom would have said twenty years ago if my light were shining in her eyes.

Suddenly I was furious with my mother for her negativity, her sarcasm and lack of appreciation. I was mad at her for not growing up enough, when she had time enough. And now it was too late.

I thought I'd learned to stop judging her, but that lesson, it seemed, needed to be applied a number of times before it would stick.

There was still time for me to grow up. Thank God.

NAKEDNESS

One Sunday morning, I opened the closet and studied my wardrobe. Today I was off to church, so I chose a long eggplant-colored skirt and a lavender tee. Mom would like the color, when I went to kiss her goodbye.

We had photos of my mother as a teenager, coquettishly posed in a bathing suit, like Greta Garbo. In another photo, she wore a voluminous red skirt and a radiant smile, arms demurely clasped behind her back. She relished the power of sky-blue eyes, a C cup and a pair of shapely gams.

Nowadays, a dozen tee shirts and pajama tops hung in her closet. We rotated through these in about a week and a half. No pants, no skirts, no shoes or socks. She lay on the bed in her Depends and tee, naked legs jutting like fence posts across the mattress. When Claire and I went to change her, we would shut the door, draw the curtains, and turn off the video monitor before pulling off the blankets.

Today at church I tuned out the sermon and read parts of Genesis. I closed my eyes and saw two men carrying a blanket. Walking backwards, they entered a tent and, faces averted, spread it over their elderly father, who was insensible with drink. Old Noah, that faithful preacher of righteousness, lay exposed, the subject of Ham's mockery.

But Shem and Japheth hid their father's shame. They may have thought, *There go I.*

The Bible depicts humans as made in the image of God, but after the sin of Adam and Eve we lost our glory. We became fallen eternal spirits living in wattle-and-daub huts. My mother was so naked. Her muscles and fat had melted away, exposing bone and sinew.

We were all made of meat, in various stages of rottenness. Our only hope was that the God who told us the story of Adam and Eve had also told us the gospel, which promised a day when He would permanently, gloriously, cover our nakedness.

I considered this often when Claire and I snapped on our exam gloves, cleaned, changed, turned and covered. We took off the gloves, smoothed the blankets and thought, *There go I.*

GRIM RESOLVE

*W*ith Claire and Arthur on vacation, it was just me and Cassidy and Nifo. Mom hadn't moved her bowels for quite a while in spite of a double dose of laxative, so I decided to go all out. For some reason, she was now able to handle chewy and crunchy foods, so for breakfast I gave her dried apricots, a piece of bacon, a tiny pancake with flax seeds, and some fully-caffeinated black sweet tea. And awaited the outcome with grim resolve.

When I first started mulling the feasibility of caring for Mom at home, she could toilet herself. I imagined any future difficulties would present themselves as Mom wandering, forgetting to turn off the stove, or developing a nasty temper. In my weirdest dreams I never imagined changing my mother's diaper.

When we hired the caregivers, we prayed that Mom's bowels would move only while the professionals were there to clean it up. We used the code phrase, "Nifo earned her pay today" to mean that the unfortunate caregiver had had to deal with the ghastly results of Mom's daily dose of senna.

One day Mom needed a change when no caregivers were present. I offered to hoist her onto her side so Claire could focus on the dirty work. I was the stronger one, after all.

Good old Claire. She was a big believer in cleanliness. We began measuring the size of the bowel movement by the number of wipes required to remove it.

Then the day came when there was no one home but me and Mom, and I did it alone, because I had to. I'll be honest. It wasn't my best work. But it was good enough.

Sometimes I lay in bed as the residual odors wafted through the darkness, wondering, *What is it like for people who do this with no help?* All over the world, I thought, there are men and women lying in the darkness, breathing in the odor of feces, haunted by the uncomprehending expression in the eyes of a spouse, lover, parent or grandparent.

There were many, many people who soldiered on, loving quietly and persistently. They had given up careers, travel, freedom. But God saw and remembered. I was sure of it.

GOD SPEAKS IN A WEST AFRICAN DIALECT

One weekend I took an entire Saturday to attend a conference. Claire and Arthur were out of town, so I engaged caregivers from morning to night.

When I came home, Nifo was beaming. "I put Ginny in the wheelchair and took her all around the house. She sat on the porch for three hours. She listened to the birds. She felt the breeze on her face. I could tell. She was so happy she was almost crying."

Mom had been saying every day for weeks that she wanted to "get out of here." Now, she had done it. I hurried to her room and asked, "How are you?"

"I'm okay," she responded dully.

"What did you do today?" I hinted, smiling.

"I was just lying here all day."

Why did I keep forgetting that she forgot? If she kept forgetting, why did we try so hard to make her life nice?

At dinner, Mom insisted on eating her nightly pharmaceutical/ice cream amalgamation without any help. The bowl lurched in her unsteady hand, and drug-impregnated meltage dripped onto her bony ribcage. A chunk of solid ice cream plopped onto her shirt. I snatched the bowl back, grabbed the chunk before it could melt further, then deftly spooned the remaining medicine/dessert into her mouth.

"How did that happen?" asked Mom. "How did I make such a mess? I didn't do that," she insisted as I briskly wiped her face, hands and shirt with a wet washcloth.

I decided not to engage, but moved on to tooth-brushing, diaper-changing and turning. I covered her with blankets, hugged her and told her I loved her. She sneered, "Yeah, I could tell all evening."

Why did she remember my brusque ministrations, but not the Glorious Afternoon on the Porch?

Later, I lay in the dark and wondered desperately, *How can I succeed at this?*

The following morning I was glad to go to church. The speaker was an evangelist from West Africa. Kwame told of his family's deep roots in Islam, his curiosity about somebody named Jesus, and recurrent visions of this Jesus who kept reaching out to him.

Kwame told his audience how he finally went to the home of a Christian to ask about these visions. There he found only the man's wife, who did not speak his language. When he asked her about Jesus, she understood him in her language, and when she explained, he heard her in his language. This miraculous bilingual conversation resulted in his conversion.

But his conversion resulted in his father's decision to kill him. And when Kwame's mother, for the only time in her life, stood up to her husband, saying, "If you kill him, you will have to kill me first," his father relented. "I will not kill you," he declared. "But you will be in our house as a slave. You are no longer my son."

The entire sanctuary was still. I felt tears rising.

Kwame labored as a slave in his own house for five years. He was forbidden to eat at the family table, but did all the work, under the cloud of his father's disapproval.

One day, he said, he came home from church and found the entire family weeping. His father said, "I was wrong. You do not have to be a slave any more."

After the service I remained seated, head bowed, hands knotted in my lap, while the other churchgoers filed out. I remembered Jesus asking, "Will you do this for Me?" I had focused on the "do this" part. I forgot the "for Me" part.

*Inasmuch as ye have done it unto one of the least
of these my brethren, ye have done it unto me.*

— MATTHEW 25:40

At home in the laundry room, I noticed Mom's shirts were mottled brown in front. I got out the stain remover and started spraying and scrubbing. This time I was doing it for Jesus.

NOTHING TO SAY

One morning while Claire was out of town, my mother woke up in a pool of urine. The catheter was leaking again. This time she was soaked all the way up her back. The job was too big for me. I called Nifo and asked her to come in early. I changed Mom's briefs and waited, feeling soiled on her behalf.

Years ago, when my babies woke with wet pajamas, I was keen to get them into the tub immediately. I wanted to put Mom into the bath and lather her up so she smelled like baby shampoo. But of course this was impossible.

As I sat with her, she said, "I feel so helpless."

"Nifo will be here in half an hour, and she'll clean you up and change your sheets and everything."

"What do I do in the meantime?"

"You can watch TV, or do your puzzle, listen to music, or read these Reader's Digests," I suggested.

"...Or you could sit and talk to me."

I laughed uncomfortably. "I don't have anything to say." This was not true. I always had something to say. But not to my mother because we didn't converse. We just took turns saying things.

If Claire were there, I might have shared something fascinating from my psychology text. But this would only confuse Mom, and might even upset her.

If I were with a friend, I might ask about her plans for the day, how things were going in general, or what she's been reading. None of these questions could be used to facilitate conversation with Mom. She had no plans and she didn't read. I imagined her thoughts squeezing slowly, one at a time, through a small opening. By the time one got through, the others had evaporated.

Nifo arrived, and soon Mom was in a clean shirt. As Nifo made the bed with fresh linens, she and I chatted about the yard, the weeds, the cost of water. We didn't have to think of things to say. We each had a store of thoughts and experiences from which to draw, and we exchanged them as naturally as two baseball players warming up with a game of catch. After I left Mom to Nifo's care, they lapsed into silence. The next time I passed Mom's room, I heard only the raucous sounds of *The Price Is Right* on the TV.

LOVE PRESSES ON

JUNE 2014

*N*ifo was talking to Claire in the hallway. "Her dementia is getting worse," she said in her musical Samoan lilt. "She just tried to hit me. She threw her water at me and called me a bitch. Now I have to change her sheets because they're all wet." She spoke matter-of-factly, but Claire and I were horrified. Mom, violent and profane? I went in to help.

Mom had arrested Nifo's hands and was squeezing them in a death grip. Nifo disentangled one hand, and Mom turned her attention to me. She pinched my wrist. Hard. "Mom," I commanded, "stop pinching me." She mouthed, eyes wide, "Help me."

I leaned down to put my ear near her mouth. "They're going to kill me. They said they were going to kill me," she whispered fiercely.

"Who?"

"Them," she hissed, darting her eyes toward Nifo, who was rolling up the damp sheet. Now Mom was clutching the rails with both hands. "Don't let them kill me," she begged.

"No one will kill you, Mom. I won't let them." I pried her fingers from the bar carefully. Her skin was so fragile. Now Nifo was deftly sliding a dry sheet under Mom's side. We turned her slowly, then pulled the sheet under and tucked it in on the other side.

Nifo proceeded to change Mom's shirt. She cajoled sweetly, "Come on, Ginny. We'll change your shirt and then you can have your dinner."

"Oh, I can have my dee-ner," Ginny mocked, her eyes widening in my direction, as if we were sharing an inside joke. "'Change your shirt and you can have your *dee-ner.*'"

Nifo dumped the wet things into the laundry basket. Mom struggled to raise her body up, to heft her skeletal legs over the railing. I stood back a minute, just to see if she could do it. But even with the adrenaline rush, she couldn't get even one leg over.

"Mom, Mom," I soothed, pulling her down onto the mattress with a hug. "Don't go away now. Nothing bad will happen to you. I won't let anything happen."

Nifo's shift was over. As she collected her things to leave, I took her aside to apologize. She waved me away. "She's not so bad. I've seen much worse."

Well, I hadn't. As Nifo left, she called out, "Goodbye." And Mom shouted weakly after her, "Shut up."

My mother had been unfailingly, and at times gratingly,

polite all my life. How could I love this person who seemed not even to be my mother any more?

She couldn't be trained, taught, or reasoned with. She could only be loved. There was nothing --*nothing*-- I could do to rescue her. I'd walked this path before, and not so long ago. My heart had already been broken. You trust a person, you love a person, and then they change. You try everything till there's nothing left to try. Then you learn to forgive. Return a blessing. Seek peace and pursue it. Love doesn't have adrenaline to give it a rush of strength which dissipates when the crisis is over. It just presses on.

THE BLUE ROCKING CHAIR

JUNE 1966
QUANTICO, VIRGINIA

I can't sleep. I hear the television down the hall in the living room, where I know my parents are reading, my father in his recliner and my mother in the blue upholstered rocking chair. Occasionally they glance up, he from the newspaper and she from a novel, and attend to whatever is on the TV --probably the news, or a movie.

I slide off the bed, and slip a little as the soles of my footie pajamas hit the hardwood floor. I drag my blanket out into the hallway and peep around the corner till my mother spies me. "I can't sleep," I whimper.

She smiles and opens her arms to receive me up into her lap. Her body is warm and soft, and she smells sweetly of Jergens hand lotion. My ear is pressed to her chest, and through her body I hear the rocking chair's ka-dunk, ka-dunk, ka-dunk. She runs her fingertips lightly across my forehead to smooth the hair from my eyes. Her lips brush the top of my head as I drift off to sleep.

She was the person who got me a drink of water or changed my diaper or dried my tears. She was the one who drove me to parties and practices, did my laundry, paid the bills, played Rummy with me. She taught me to sew, make my bed, bake cookies and do small repairs around the house. She took care of me when I was sick. Before computers, she typed letters. Before GPS, she mapped out a route. Mom bowled, mowed and trimmed, vacuumed, brought in the groceries, drove across state line after state line.

She even took me fishing, and cleaned and cooked the fish.

I have forgotten all these things, because the person beside me bears no resemblance to the woman who raised me. I have been angry with Mom since 4:00am. It's now 10:30am, and I lie here praying at the ceiling. I tell God how mad I am, that I have no right to hold anything against Mom. But who can I hold it against?

She stirred in the wee hours, and then just kept stirring. She rattled the bed rails, clutched at the bedside table, talked nonsense, and tried to seize an imagined item. I woke, fell asleep, woke again. I adjusted her bedclothes, gave her water, answered her questions. Finally I just got up, opened the curtains and called it a morning.

It seems so pointless. Did my attempts to make her feel comfortable, loved and safe make any difference? And if they made a difference this morning, do they make a difference now? She's forgotten the whole thing.

But I remember being four years old, cuddled up in her arms in the blue rocking chair.

MORE BLESSED

JULY 2014/JANUARY 1963

I left Claire to keep an eye on Mom while I flew to Illinois for the birth of Rebekah's baby. Fortunately, Mom continued to sleep through the night. Claire and Arthur, the lark and the owl, took their turns checking up on her, he during the late night hours and she in the early morning.

In the summer of 1963, First Lieutenant Keith Soesbe and his very pregnant wife were getting ready for bed when Ginny was astonished to discover warm water pooling at her feet. She grabbed onto the edge of the dresser and leaned forward, legs apart. For a few seconds, they watched the clear fluid spread out across the linoleum.

"I think it's time," she said.

Keith and Ginny lived in Officers' housing on base, so it

didn't take long to reach the Naval Hospital. At the check-in, Ginny said with some urgency, "The baby's coming."

"Of course the baby's coming," the receptionist assured her.

"I mean the baby's coming *now*."

While Keith was showing the receptionist his ID card, signing papers, filling out forms, Ginny tried not to cry out. Soon she was being trundled toward the elevator in a wheelchair.

"The baby's coming," she repeated.

"Yes," smiled the orderly. "We're getting you right up to Labor and Delivery."

Keith was left in the waiting room. In the obstetrics unit, a nurse helped the orderly lift Ginny onto a bed.

The nurse lifted my mother's gown. "Oh my God," she cried. "The baby's coming."

So, at a time when twilight sleep was still in use, before Lamaze and Bradley brought us back to nature's way, I made my hasty debut with no drugs and no cutting. We were all taken aback.

Rebekah's baby, however, was in no such hurry. While my daughter labored endlessly, I paced about the Chicago Medical District, seeing nothing and constantly checking my phone for updates.

This was taking a long time. Should I get a sandwich for Josh? I saw a sub shop in the distance and decided to decide on the way. It was a hot day, and I could use an unsweetened tea with plenty of ice.

I passed an elderly woman on a bench. She called out,

"Do you have money so I can buy a sandwich?" She was missing several teeth.

I had a policy: No money. "No," I responded reflexively, without stopping.

And yet. And yet. The Holy Spirit recently pointed out to me something Jesus said, and it kept coming up: "Give to everyone who asks of you, and whoever takes away what is yours, do not demand it back." I had parsed and prayed. I had balanced my wish for a generous and loving heart with the wish to not contribute to anyone's delinquency or to be taken advantage of. So the second part of the policy was: Give what you can, give what they need.

I got a foot long ham sub and two drinks. On the way back I approached her. "Do you like lemonade?"

Her face lit up. "Oh, God bless you! Thank you."

I sat on the bench beside her and asked, "Do you like ham?"

"Sure."

I extracted half the sandwich from its plastic housing and gave her the rest. Smiling, she tucked the whole thing into a bag at her feet, still enthusiastically nursing the cup of lemonade.

As I unwrapped my half, I asked, "Where do you live?"

"On the street. I'll take this back with me to the shelter."

We chatted amiably. I finished my lunch, and presently felt I must be getting back to the hospital.

On the walk back I pondered her situation. She was daily in need of food, water, shelter, clothing. She couldn't make or buy these things for herself. *What is it like,* I wondered, *to have to ask for everything?*

Like Mom.

I preferred to be the one who gave, rather than the one who had to ask. Someday, I may be the one asking. I hoped whoever heard my request had not only a sound policy, but a generous and loving heart. And maybe some time to sit and listen.

REGRET

JULY 2014/JULY 1984
CHICAGO, ILLINOIS/WACO, TEXAS

*B*aby Marshall arrived the following day, to everyone's joy and relief. *If only Mom could hold him*, I thought.

In July of 1984, my grandmother suffered a devastating stroke. Mom flew to Texas immediately. She called the next day in tears and said it was bad. Granny was unable to talk or respond. She was alive, but that was all.

"Should I go out to see her?" I asked. I was eight months pregnant. Would I be allowed to get on a plane?

"I don't think so, Susan. She wouldn't even know you're here. And how can you fly in your condition?"

So I didn't go. Benjamin was born in December, and Granny lingered until August of 1985.

I wish I had gone in his early months. I would have laid little Benjamin down on Granny's chest, and she would have smelled his fuzzy little head, and known we were there. She would know I hadn't forgotten her. Wisdom comes too late.

FULL CIRCLE

AUGUST 2014
KLAIPEDA, LITHUANIA

*I*n August, Deborah arrived at the Amazingly Large House with her few belongings. She would take my place caring for Mom while I was in Europe. I flew east to help Benjamin and Corrie wrangle their two young children on the sixteen-hour trip to Lithuania.

The weather in the port city of Klaipeda was balmy, and the summer days were long. That first night, I slept in a windowless room. In the wee hours I lurched out of bed to comfort Elizabeth, who had awakened in a strange new place.

Elizabeth was a serious thirteen-month-old with eyes like two bright buttons. Her face was almost a perfect sphere, and when she smiled, a deep dimple appeared on each fat cheek. She wasn't sure she liked me. When her parents took her brother out later that day and left her with me in the small apartment, she looked after them and cried.

I was set to spend ten days with Benjamin and Corrie, helping them settle into their apartment which looked out over a small pond populated with swans. Slowly, we all got used to the time change and the sporadic rainfall.

Deborah wrote to me,

```
Things are going really well. I try to help
sometimes by holding Grandma's hand and making
her laugh. And rubbing her shoulder. I don't
know how helpful I am at night prep, but at
least Aunt Claire feels less alone, hopefully.
She is definitely more stressed without you,
but that could have been because of the dog not
taking her pills, and then pooping all over the
house. That really brought Claire down. But I
helped as much as I could with all that.
```

Benjamin and Corrie took Daniel for a bike ride. In my arms, Elizabeth whimpered, leaning toward the front door. I wanted to redirect her to a happier place, so I took her out to see the swans. We sat on the cement bench, and I spoke of swans and water and sunshine. Her body relaxed against mine as she sucked thoughtfully on her binky. The land seemed to be breathing the sun-cleansed air, exhaling its sweetness over us. She rested in my lap, her little fingers running up and down the back of my arm. Elizabeth's hair smelt of baby, and love was coursing through my limbs and pooling in my chest. I ran my fingertips lightly across her forehead to smooth the hair from her eyes.

I never loved a child until I had my own. My attachment to all my babies was instant and feral. The grandchildren were different. I hadn't carried them; they didn't smell like me. I loved Daniel and Elizabeth by faith, and we were growing into each other. I wondered if my mother's mother felt that way about me.

Every summer, Claire and I would stay at our grandmother's little pink and white house in Waco for weeks. At family dinners, where we and our cousins were seated at a table separate from the adults, Granny assuaged our humiliation by joining us and acting silly. She always had something for her grandchildren to play with, some project we could join in. At Granny's the children were included in the card games and allowed to eat the bridge mix. She paid attention to us. She made us all feel that we were worth spending time with, worth spending money on. We all knew Granny was there for us, a very present help in time of trouble.

I knew now that she was laying a foundation. She created a place we could repair to when life knocked us down. Granny was our rock. She prayed for us. Jesus was her rock. Now He was mine.

I pulled Elizabeth a little closer and kissed her fuzzy baby head. Life is hard and problems come. I prayed, *Jesus, be her rock.*

LETTING GO

It was my last day in Lithuania. Tomorrow I would board a plane for Copenhagen. I loved the idea of further adventures, but hated leaving Daniel and Elizabeth. How old would they be when I saw them next? Would they remember me? How could I let them go?

I imagined myself on a mountaintop. Behind and before me the path fades into the distance. My grandmother's and mother's paths began before mine, ran alongside it, and intersected it for a while. When did our paths diverge? That day in the driveway? Or later, after my last visit to the house in Lake Forest? When would I have said goodbye to my mother over these last ten years? And what about Granny? What did I say to her the last time we saw each other, that last day in the pink and white house in Waco? When I turned and walked down the front steps, I didn't know I would never see her again.

Looking down the path ahead of me, I saw my mother's

timeline coming to an end. Mine, too, stopped somewhere down there in the misty valley. Would my children's and grandchildren's footprints criss-cross my path? Would there be time to lay a foundation? And how could I know I was leaving them a legacy worthy of Granny?

PERSPECTIVE

*Y*ou can't spend all that money for a plane ticket and see only one country. On the way back to California, I stopped to spend a few days in Denmark. From a tiny modern hostel room in Copenhagen I tapped out a text to Claire:

Woke refreshed in my cubicle, had a hearty breakfast and plan to be out all day on a tour, museum visit and canal boat ride. Have a great day!

She responded:

Deborah and I were met with a twenty-five-wipe poop last night. Also we had to deal with Boost that Mom had spilled in her bed. When we were done cleaning up, Mom asked why it had taken so long. We just laughed.

I laughed too, grateful they could both take it in stride. I wondered if Claire had discovered the picture of Jack Ma I had taped up in her side of the pantry before I left.

GIFTS MY MOTHER GAVE ME

WALDANGELLOCH, GERMANY

The next leg of my journey took me to Germany, so I spent a few days in a small village on the outskirts of Frankfurt. My hostess suggested a bicycle ride, so I took to the trails with dense brown bread, tart little apples and a block of Emmentaler cheese in my backpack. Oh, and my Kindle.

As I cycled past the quaint beauties of Waldangelloch's forests and fields, my heart swelled with gratitude for a mellow childhood. I was only expected to attend school every day (unless verifiably ill), make no trouble and bring home nothing less than all A's. This, it turned out, was not all that hard. And when school was out, I could do as I liked. I rolled down grass-covered hills with my friends and gamboled about the little pockets of wilderness in our neighborhood, poking into drainage ditches and turning over rocks. My summers were long and leisurely. When we weren't in Texas, my sister and I were at home enjoying the extravagant freedom afforded us by bikes and books, bounded only by a curfew and a modicum of chores.

Claire and I read a lot. Our parents, too, were always reading. Books were stacked up on bedside tables, coffee tables, the back of the toilet, the kitchen table. Dad pored over magazines and Vietnam War books and *The Whole Earth Catalog*; Mom read mysteries and romance and historical fiction. We read in our own rooms, in the living room, at the table and in the yard.

Mom took us to the library every week, where we returned a stack of books and eagerly selected a fresh batch. Our mother, who hated to spend money on anything, shocked us by letting us join the Scholastic Book Club at school and buying us *as many books as we wanted at full price*. Such unexpected extravagance! When the teacher passed out the order form, I took it home and checked the boxes for all the books which caught my fancy. Mom sent me back to school with an envelope containing the exact amount of money required. She bought me books about dogs and horses and homework machines; witches and quirky relatives; contraptions and inventions; bullies and mysteries, stories which involved chemistry sets and talking animals. Stories took me to other times and places while I was safe on my bed or lying on the grass in the back yard.

A stone wall encircled a shady park just off Michelfelder Straße. I leaned the borrowed bike against a thick tree and scrambled up the wall. I sprawled on the broad copestone, munched apples and read Thomas

Mann's *Royal Highness*. On the way back, I stopped at a sandwich shop for a bottle of beer. Two Turkish men regarded me with undisguised curiosity as I tucked it into my backpack. Pre-dementia Mom would not approve of the beer, but she would have asked me to tell her about *Royal Highness*. I wished I could.

THE LONG VIEW

SEPTEMBER 2014

*N*ine months after we moved into the Amazingly Large House, Claire and I sat down to calculate our monthly expenditure on caregivers, and agreed the current outlay was unsustainable. Much as we loved Nifo, we couldn't afford to pay agency rates any longer. We decided to replace her with a caregiver we could employ privately. Claire, Deborah and I would increase the number of hours we tended Mom.

This was getting complicated. We posted a big erasable calendar board in the kitchen, and used colored markers to keep everybody's schedule straight.

Linda on SitterCity agreed to an interview. She was a willowy woman in her sixties, dressed in cheerful colors, long palomino hair in a ponytail. We struck a deal, and began adding her name to the big calendar.

A GOOD LIFE

OCTOBER 2014

*M*om used to ask for dark chocolate, and then she forgot to. For a while I was glad because candy wasn't exactly a healthy choice. But I started bringing her chocolates again. Hospice may focus on helping patients experience a good death, but in the meantime I wanted Mom to have a good life.

In between school and feeding Mom chocolates, I worked on what I called The Photo Project: thirty years of family photographs to be culled, arranged, labeled and digitized. I got a deal for the scanning, and thank God, because the sorting part was taking forever.

When the marital assets were divided I got the photos. Scanning and digitizing would help the kids and me remember the good times. It would help us heal. I could have let the pain overspread the past and stain it with bitterness, but I wanted to avoid that unholy intinction.

The divorce didn't invalidate everything. I figured my children should see these artifacts and know that our family began well and ran smoothly for quite a while.

Amongst the pictures of birthdays, field trips and just clowning around were photos of our family of six spending a month each winter with my parents in their smallish house in Lake Forest. When the children were little, we all stayed in the guest room. Later, when Dad bought a camping trailer and parked it next to the house, the children slept in it. They loved that. And Dad was pleased that they were so easily pleased.

Every year before we came I sent Mom an extensive grocery list, and she bought everything on it without question. Her deal was, "I shop, you cook." I didn't mind. I liked cooking.

Mom did all our laundry for the whole month. She washed the dishes and the clothes, and I washed the children.

My husband Ralph couldn't join us for a whole month in California, so Mom watched the kids while I got a perm. I met with my friends and took walks, knowing the children were safe and happy with Mom. The photos showed trips to Legoland, Disneyland, the San Juan Capistrano Mission, camping trips, tide pooling. The only compensation my parents got was the pleasure of our company. They weren't much for going out, and they needed nothing. They didn't expect gifts or outings. Once or twice we took them to Sizzler, the one restaurant they enjoyed because of its vast all-you-can-eat selection.

I needed to see these pictures again. I needed to

remember who Mom was and what she did for me. She not only birthed and nurtured me. She tried, in her way, to give me a good life. She didn't demand. She gave. She opened her home, loved me as I was, did what she could.

After I left home and married, she carried on, pursuing her middle-aged pursuits. When I called to tell her we were getting divorced, she said, "Oh, Susan." When times were tough, she sent me "loans" which she later quietly forgave. When Dad got sick, I flew out for visits. We were there for each other, but I couldn't make a life for her any more than she could make a life for me.

When I wondered if it was a waste of time trying to give Mom a good life as she lay in her bed, I remembered that she tried to give me a good life. I couldn't make everything okay for her. And she couldn't make everything okay for me. But wasn't it nice that we could give it a good shot, each in our turn? Wasn't that just love?

MOURNING

On Halloween a doctor from hospice came to check on Mom for recertification. When I asked how Mom looked to her, she glanced at me quizzically. "Oh, she's recertified all right." Her tone and expression said "Duh."

I walked into the room and found my sister trying to brush Mom's teeth. Claire stood with her fist on her hip. "I can't believe it," she exclaimed, "She can't even swish the water around in her mouth and spit. She just swallowed it down."

I thought, *What did you expect?*

Claire went on, "I had to throw away her electric tooth-brush, the one she was so excited about when I first bought it for her. Just seeing it there in the trash...." She looked away. We tried not to cry in front of each other.

When the exciting new WaterPik came out in the 1970s, our penny-pinching mother happily bought one for us. As recently as a few years ago, she expressed pride in the fact that she still had all her teeth. Now there just wasn't enough of Mom left to care.

That night Claire and I sat on the deck drinking tea and recalling things Mom used to do. She said, "I took Mom to a doctor when she lived at Omnia. In the waiting room, I had to put down my book to engage her in conversation. I wondered then why she hadn't brought a book. That's when I discovered she'd stopped reading."

When we weren't looking, that part fell off, another autumn leaf drifting lazily to the forest floor. Claire was mourning the losses piece by piece, as they became too obvious to ignore. I was putting off mourning, telling myself that sadness accomplishes nothing. Sometimes it punched its way out, though, and I had to pull off the freeway and have a good, blinding cry. But I would always drive home afterwards and walk into Mom's room with a smile. She didn't know what she had lost, and she wasn't mourning at all.

FEEDING MOM

NOVEMBER 2014

One Saturday morning I ran into Claire coming out of Mom's room. Her expression told me she needed someone to run interference. I asked, "Should I make Mom breakfast?"

"Well, I gave her a banana and she's just holding it."

Yes, Mom is clutching a chunk of naked banana in her clawlike hand. She looks at me expectantly. Claire brings in applesauce and pills: two for pain, two for regularity, one for mood.

I pry the banana out of Mom's fist and toss it onto the bedside tray. I bury the pain pills in a spoonful of applesauce, send up a prayer for a smooth journey and lift the spoon to her lips.

She takes the applesauce well enough, but works the pills up onto the tip of her tongue, then brings her forefinger and thumb up to her mouth as if to remove and discard the pills. "No," I say. "Eat them. Swallow those down." I don't usually issue commands like this, but I'm not in the mood to think of new ways to spirit the drugs into her bloodstream. I pull her hand gently away from her face.

She finishes that mouthful and I quickly embed the remaining medications into spoonfuls of applesauce. Even the senna laxative pills, which are fat and bitter tasting, go down without any resistance. She crunches the disgusting admixture and looks perplexed. The meds down, now I can concentrate on calories.

How many calories does an eighty-pound woman need, whose sole activities are chewing and pooping? Not many. Still, getting them in is an arduous task.

I scoop a small chunk of banana onto the spoon and lift it up where she can see it. She asks, "What is that?"

"It's a piece of banana."

"What am I supposed to do?

"Eat it," I say, commanding again. "Put it into your mouth and swallow it down." I left out the part about the chewing. I hope it's okay.

"It doesn't look... mouthy," she observes.

"It's okay."

"Are you sure?"

"Yes, I'm sure."

She eats it. She chews the banana slowly and thoroughly, as if it were a piece of steak.

A few minutes later I repeat my offer of a teaspoon-sized morsel of banana. She's staring out the window.

When she finally focuses on the food she asks, "What's that?"

"A piece of banana."

She laughs. "You kill me." But she eats it. Another marathon of chewing and swallowing ensues. I sit back and wait, gathering up patience like a cloak over my shoulders. I have all day. I have all week. All eternity, if necessary. To do this one thing, right now, is all there is.

The next time I offer banana, she asks, "Is this more pig?"

"No, it's banana."

"You sure about that?"

"Yes, I'm sure."

She eats, chewing unhurriedly. She points vaguely in the direction of the foot of the bed. "Is that one, over there?" she asks.

"Is that one what?"

"Is that an egg?"

"Where?"

"Over in the corner."

"I see pillows in the corner," I report. "Not an egg. Have some banana." She opens wide.

In this way I feed my mother half a banana and two tablespoons of applesauce in forty-five minutes.

SAFE FROM ALL HARM

OCTOBER 1939
TEXAS

Three-year-old Ginny was standing in the wagon when the mule lurched forward, causing her to plop down hard on the wooden seat. A boil on her left buttock burst, and pain shot through her body. She felt the hot fluid soaking through her panties and dress. She stifled a cry, but tears sprang up. Mama shaded her eyes with the back of her hand and squinted up at her little girl. "Are you all right, sweetheart?"

Ginny gripped the edge of the seat with both hands and declared, "I'm all right." Mama moved off to pick more cotton under the blazing Texas sun. The field was thick with snowy white bolls, and Mama and Daddy picked as quickly as they could, their calloused fingers stuffing boll after boll into the sacks slung over their stooped shoulders.

At night, Ginny lay on a blanket bed between Mama and Daddy, and stared up through the clear air at the stars twinkling miles above. Finally, it was cool enough to sleep. She tried not to imagine the shadowy monsters which were surely lurking in the dark, past the blanket's edge. The bed was safe. If she kept within its perimeter she would, magically, remain unharmed.

METHADONE VS SENNA

*R*achel sat at the dining room table, hands poised over the keyboard, deliberating with herself about whether or not to increase Ginny's daily methadone dose.

"Why is this a big deal?" I asked, tapping a pen on the spiral bound journal before me. "If Mom needs more pain meds, why not just give them to her?"

"Methadone and morphine trigger constipation."

"That doesn't sound too bad," I laughed. "It's better than diarrhea, isn't it?"

"Not exactly. Bowel impaction can kill a person. We have to keep her bowels moving regularly or she could be in trouble."

Years ago, Claire and I made a trip to the Mütter Museum in Philadelphia, where we saw, among other remarkable medical oddities, something labeled the "Giant Megacolon." About the size of a stout ten-year-old, it once belonged to a man who suffered from a condition which made him unable to move his bowels. This picture flashed through my mind as I responded hastily, "Of course."

Never before had I thought so much about bowel movements: their frequency, consistency, and volume. I installed a daily logbook in Mom's room to keep a record of them. Linda kept meticulous records of medicines and outputs in old-school cursive, and Cassidy made us laugh out loud with her description: "A whole rotisserie chicken from Costco."

Finally Rachel decided to order more methadone. "You have enough senna, right? Good. See you next Thursday."

GATHERING THOUGHTS

One day Mom actually got mail. "Look, Mom," I said, waving the envelope before her. "Cousin Rosemary sent you a card."

Mom said, "Aren't you going to bring me candy?"

I said, "First, take a look at this." She studied the card for a long time, trying to gather thoughts that never came.

Have you ever forgotten something, and stood still, your eyes traveling back and forth over your immediate surroundings as you try mightily to make the forgotten thing appear? It's right there, just around the corner. You feel it approaching. If you wait long enough, it will show itself. I imagined that's how it was for a person with advanced dementia. Waiting, waiting, for the information to arrive any second now. Like the spinning beach ball of death.

Sometimes I walked into a room and forgot what I came for. I retraced my steps, and it came back to me. I forgot people's names, and looked for them in my address book, or I asked someone. What if one day the information I want simply wasn't there anymore?

Some theorize that Alzheimer's is a sort of diabetes of the brain. My friend Cindy, who works with the elderly, told me, "My old people need someone to steer them away from the dessert table or they'll eat seven donuts." When I eat sugar, I wondered, am I contributing to my own dementia? Could I give up sugar if I tried? If I couldn't, did that mean I really did already have dementia and was addicted to sugar?

Mom was still holding the card, but her hand was resting on the covers, as she gazed at empty air. "I'd love to have some chocolate right about now," she hinted. I got her some.

THROUGH REBEKAH'S EYES

DECEMBER 2014

*R*ebekah and Josh joined us for Christmas, bringing baby Marshall. The eight of us squeezed into Mom's room to celebrate. Claire brought out the song sheets, and Joel fired up his guitar. Arthur's strong bass joined Deborah's and Claire's soprano on the melody line, so I added harmony as well as I could. As we sang, I scanned the room with pleasure. Most of my loved ones were there, worshipping God together. My eye stopped at Rebekah, tears spilling down her cheeks. She stole sideways glimpses of her gaunt grandmother, who stared vacantly at the assembled family. Poor Rebekah. Deborah and I had gotten used to Mom's condition, but she hadn't. We'd learned to live with tragedy, the uninvited guest. But seeing Mom through Rebekah's eyes, I felt like crying too.

DYING WELL

MARCH 2015

*I*nflate two latex balloons. After several days, deflate them. Pull the mouths of the balloons over two broomsticks. Next, place these broomsticks side by side on a soft surface and pour chocolate pudding all over the balloons. Now, snap on some nitrile exam gloves and clean all the pudding off the latex using baby wipes. Go ahead and use all the wipes you need, but don't let the pudding get on anything. This was what it was like, sometimes, when Claire and I had given Mom a tad too much of our trusty laxative, Senna.

Mom had been bedbound for more than a year. Her buttocks were almost completely devoid of muscle and fat. The tabs of her briefs now overlapped in front.

I didn't care much anymore about the shape of my body. I was now much more interested in thinking of ways to get more muscle and thicker bones. Calcium and protein were my new best friends. As I worked on the machines at the gym, I imagined my bones getting denser and denser. Take *that*, osteoporosis!

When my father's mother was in her thirties, she jumped rope with the neighborhood girls, just for fun. Grandma was pretty darn happy, and she did whatever she pleased. She drank a full glass of milk at lunch, and had a glass of wine every afternoon. She lived, well and hearty, to the age of ninety-three.

I began to pray that instead of growing old and sick like Mom, I would grow old like Grandma. I wanted to be a mellow and contented ninety-something, then die quietly. Or maybe not so quietly. Maybe I would die heroically. That would be good. Maybe I could rescue a baby or something.

Death must come. The question is not whether or not we will die, but when and how. Why do we try so hard not to think about it?

Claire and I were helping Mom outrun the grim reaper, but we knew eventually he would catch up with her. We were standing on either side of her, like Aaron and Hur alongside Moses, holding up her hands. She was too tired and weak to hold them up herself.

I AM NOT FORGOTTEN

*E*ven after fifteen months in California, I still trotted out to the mailbox every day with a sense of anticipation. Then one fine spring day my pulse quickened when I found a package from my New Jersey friend Nina. I had a good feeling about this. I ripped it open and pulled out a gargantuan denim purse, vulgarly bedizened with varicolored sequins, embroidery and tassels. I practically screamed with laughter.

A few years ago, when Nina was shopping for a new handbag, she sought my advice. She sent links to photos of three bags she was considering. One of them was so hideous I thought it was a joke. When I told her so, she said that bag was actually her favorite, and she went ahead and bought it. Now she had a new leather bag, and the old one, in all its repulsive glory, was mine. And it was full!

I extracted item after item, exclaiming, "How much stuff is *in* here?" Claire looked up from her laptop, amused and curious, as I pulled out pieces of cast-off costume jewelry, belts, coin purses, a scarf, and spread them out on the kitchen table. Nina and I loved secondhand things, and our tastes were similar. Every item was a treasure, more so because it came from a friend who knew what made me happy, and took the trouble to send it in a big box right to my doorstep. I was loved. Oh, I was loved!

I thought very briefly of the bowerbird, and chuckled. Oh well.

GETTING OUT

*I*t was time to sell Mom's jewelry. In the back of the shop, Deborah and I took our seats opposite the jeweler, who spread the jumble of baubles on her expansive desktop. She expertly tested each piece and placed it in one of two piles: the buy pile or the junk pile. She didn't call it junk, but most of Mom's jewelry was acquired at garage sales, with dimes and quarters extracted from her little leather coin purse.

But I didn't know what was valuable and what wasn't. So here we were.

Claire and I had gathered the jewelry from little caches around Mom's house, stored away in boxes and plastic bags. I finally deposited the entire collection into a little blue valise. I felt a bit sleazy sitting here in a windowless back room and offering my mom's treasures for sale. But she couldn't enjoy them anymore. Claire and I had already taken the pieces we liked, and saved out a few for our children. The only thing left was to release them into the wild where they may again be enjoyed by somebody.

There were two timid beagles in the office, recent rescues. The little animals eyed Deborah and me with worried expressions, but eventually they ignored us.

I walked out with the unwanted items and a check for Mom's account. Deborah and I stowed the valise in the back of the car and walked to a Mexican restaurant teeming with locals. In the long line we listened to lively conversations around us and shared silent smiles. I liked to think that people were busy rescuing beagles, running errands, having lunch. It was good to hear people talking about the many and varied things they were doing. Maybe I needed to get out more.

MY MOTHER'S VOICE

MAY 2015

One evening I watched a movie while feeding Mom, coaxing her dinner down bite by agonizing bite. "Get over here," she demanded, as I stood by the bed eating my own dinner from a bright yellow bowl. "Let me see that dish."

I held it up to show her. She reached for it, but I pulled it away.

"I want to see that," she insisted.

"Well, I don't want your hands all over my food," I responded. I offered her a peanut butter cracker sandwich.

"I want some of *that*," she responded, indicating my bowl.

"It's broccoli," I countered with unassailable logic. "You don't like broccoli."

She looked at me with dagger eyes. "You should be ashamed... because of your cheating and manipulating."

In my best measured tones, I said, "I am not cheating and manipulating. I am giving you peanut butter and crackers."

She took the little sandwich and poked it clumsily into her mouth, looking sullen.

I found Deborah relaxing on the bed in what used to be Joel's room before he left for college.

"Will you hug me?" I asked, and told her what happened.

She gave me a long hug, just right. "You didn't cheat and manipulate. She's out of touch with reality. You're taking care of her."

Sometimes I needed to hear someone else say what I already knew.

"I don't know if anyone else would understand how I'm feeling right now," I plopped onto the bed and stared at the trees outside the window without seeing them.

"I bet a lot of people feel that way," Deb said. "Lots of people are taking care of someone with Alzheimer's."

She was right. Hundreds of thousands. By themselves, with a spouse or siblings, with community support or without it. They would understand.

"Maybe you should join a support group," she suggested.

Maybe I should. And yet, I didn't want to be talking and thinking about my mother quite so much. I didn't want dementia to eat up my life as well as Mom's. Maybe those other people would understand that too.

When people heard that Mom had dementia, they often asked, "Does she remember who you are?" I didn't think so.

The category of thought which contains the concept of mother and daughter had simply vanished.

But I remembered who she was.

The memories were in my brain, called up by photos, videos, or oil paintings. Audiotapes and letters preserved my mother's voice. Going through her files one day, I found a letter she wrote to the Defense Finance and Accounting Service in 2004, shortly after she moved to Texas from California. She typed,

```
Gentlemen: I am writing in desperation after
all phone calls and FAXes have not accomplished
anything, it seems.
```

She complained that the DFAS had failed to deposit funds to her account for three months, and enumerated the steps she had taken to address the situation.

She concluded crisply,

```
I have done everything short of turning
handsprings to accomplish this simple feat.
I fail to see how a simple change of
residence could possibly be the cause of so
much delay.
```

I smiled as I read this letter. That was Mom's voice. It was kind of nice to hear her making sense.

THE STRAWBERRY EXPERIMENT

FEBRUARY 1997
LAKE FOREST, CALIFORNIA

On a sunny February day Ginny came through the front door, arms loaded with boxes of fat red strawberries. "They're having a sale at Albertsons," she explained. The children were jubilant.

When we came from New Jersey, she liked to get us all our favorite foods. She also hated to waste food or money, so I made sure we ate everything. This time, no problem. Rebekah was eager to help with the preparations, so we washed, cored, and consumed an entire flat of strawberries in minutes. My father, in his recliner, looked on with amusement.

"I can't believe how fast y'all eat up all those strawberries," Mom exclaimed. She looped her purse over her arm and headed for the door, keys in hand.

"Where are you going?" I asked.

"Back to Albertsons. I want to see how many strawberries y'all can eat."

When Mom returned with a second flat, Ralph, the children and I enthusiastically polished these off as well.

Ginny wordlessly drove off to Albertson's to get a third flat. This one was only half eaten when our interest petered out, and we were done.

Recalling this incident, I didn't know if she was doing an experiment or just enjoying the spectacle of her family eating as much as we wanted. Probably both.

A PERFECT DAY

MAY 2015
COSTA MESA/VISTA,
CALIFORNIA

*C*laire and Arthur left early for Joel's graduation from the Calvary Chapel School of Worship. Deborah and I were almost ready to climb into my car and join them. For once, we were on time. We said goodbye to Mom and to the faithful Linda, who was looking forward to seeing how much healthy food she could get Mom to eat that day. As we bustled out the door, the mailman came up and handed us some letters and a package. I said, "Who's it for? What is it?"

As usual, he declined to hazard a guess.

When Deborah and I saw the return address, we looked at each other with wide eyes. "It's from *Nina*," we whispered.

Deborah swiftly put the box on the table. I ran to get scissors, hacked through the tape and flipped open the box.

As I lifted out the gauze-encased nugget within, Deborah asked breathlessly, "Is it....is it.... a *cake?*"

I made myself unwrap the dense, heavy lump slowly and carefully. A stray chocolate crumb tumbled out onto the table.

"It's a *cake!*" we cried, seizing each other's hands and dancing in a circle. We chanted, "A cake, a cake, Nina's chocolate cake!"

I got plates and silverware and cut two thick wedges. While Deborah seized the moment to put finishing touches on her makeup, I savored my piece. She savored hers in the car. "What is *in* this frosting?" she marveled.

Nina's intensely chocolate cakes, moist, dense, and spiked with full strength coffee, were regarded as the gold standard at our New Jersey church. At social events, no one else dared bring a chocolate cake lest it be compared with Nina's. A tall willowy woman of German extraction, she was renowned for her fearless and liberal use of butter. This latest specimen of her legerdemain, though not strictly fresh after a three-thousand mile journey, was still head and shoulders above any chocolate cake I had ever eaten.

On the way to Calvary Chapel in Costa Mesa, Deborah and I discussed Topics of Import, our eyes shining with the refreshment of that cake and the love it conveyed.

The graduation felt laid-back and worshipful, and we clapped, danced and ululated with joy. Afterward, Joel was happy and rather flushed. Claire and Arthur hugged their son, beaming, and posed for photos.

Our jolly party of five repaired to Umami Burger,

where we were served hipster fare by a tattooed man with a handlebar mustache, who breathlessly explained our burger options with the fervor of a sommelier proffering wine choices. Claire and I tried not to laugh at the menu, which included truffled aioli, beet infused couscous, and maple-braised bacon lardons. Oh, if only Mom could see us now! She would join in the mockage, and probably do it better than all of us.

In the car on the way home, I asked Deborah for the remains of her cake. Laughing, she stuck chunks into my mouth as I drove, because we were in a hurry to get home in time to relieve Linda. Stuffed with hamburgers and cake and happiness, we grooved to worship tunes and marveled at the chaparral and the gray-blue ocean.

Later one of Deborah's friends popped over, and we watched *National Treasure* while using the video monitor to keep an eye on Mom, who dozed peacefully.

When the movie was over, I printed out some online photos of Jack Ma and taped them up in places where Claire would find them when she returned: inside her closet, under the lid of the washing machine, on her CD player, under her pillow. I cackled gleefully all the while. Would she find any of them that night, when she and Arthur got home? Or the next morning? Or even all through the week? Imagining her response was perhaps more fun than witnessing her actual reaction.

I was particularly proud of the one in the shower, which you couldn't see till you were completely inside the stall.

All this time, Mom was content in her room. She dozed

or watched Beatrix Potter DVDs. Deborah and I changed her brief, turned her, tucked her in without incident. I smoothed her hair back from her forehead, and said, as if telling her a secret, "Mama is making pecan pie in the kitchen. The sky is big and blue, with billowy clouds, and the bluebonnets are in bloom."

She sighed and closed her eyes. Drifting off, she drawled in a whisper, "I played outside."

It was a perfect day.

CLOUDS

*I*n late May, Cassidy called me into Mom's room to show me a smallish blood clot in the catheter bag, and something else floating at the top which could have been a lilliputian jellyfish. I wondered again what was going on inside Mom's body. What were those organs doing? Shutting down? Gearing up? Coping bravely? Did "business as usual" include a blood clot? Rachel made a note of it, but declined further action.

~

A FEW DAYS later I texted Rachel in the early morning hours,

Mom is uncharacteristically awake and making
groaning noises. Can you come ASAP?

Rachel responded quickly:

Give her a dose of morphine and Lorazepam.
Dissolve in half syringe water and put under her
tongue. I will be there ASAP.

And she was. We didn't know what was distressing
Mom, but apparently the meds brought relief. By the time
Cassidy arrived at 9:00am, Mom was back to what was, for
her at least, normal.

For a little while I forgot that my mother was dying.
The clouds had receded and the sun shone, and everything
felt balanced. But you have to focus to maintain balance,
and sometimes you have to reach out and grab the person
next to you. Rachel was there to be grabbed. I forgot about
her, too, but she knew I'd be reaching out again sooner
or later.

Meanwhile, on the front lines, Cassidy fielded a bowel
movement which she recorded lyrically in the logbook as
"like Mount Vesuvius, and my hand was Pompeii."

FELLOWSHIP

I hadn't really made any connections at church, but to be honest, I wasn't trying that hard. Now, selfishly, I felt I needed to get out there more. I seized the opportunity to attend a cooking class and Bible study in Valley Center. Everybody else knew where Valley Center was, but not me. So the pastor's wife arranged a ride for me with Roxie, a slender, fifty-something blonde lady in high heels. *California is the land of granola and Birkenstocks*, I sighed inwardly. *Why do the women in church wear heels and do up their hair?* I was so tired of feeling like a Cabbage Patch Kid in the land of Barbies.

In the parking lot after church I climbed into Roxie's gold-tone sedan and kicked off my flats. She asked me what I did, and I told her. She nodded and said, "Just last year my mother-in-law died. I've spent the last ten years caring for my parents and my in-laws. They all had dementia, except Mom."

Roxie listened quietly as I shared my joys and struggles. I was surprised at how much gut I spilled. But she wasn't. Roxie knew a thing or two about loving people.

This woman was no mere Barbie doll. She was a kickass caregiver. When would I finally learn to stop judging by appearances?

CLEANSED

JUNE 2015

In June, I completed another twelve-week block of online classes. After triumphantly hitting the "submit" button on the final exam, I booked a flight to New Jersey. It was a bit late for a brisk walk on the beach, but being suddenly unshackled made me giddy, so I climbed into the car and went anyway.

Vista was arid and cloudless, like a desert. At midday, the sun's rays baked the sidewalks. At night, the heat dissipated in the thin atmosphere. But at the beach the air was gravid, carrying the smell of salt water, of sunshine, of living things and dead things. The contrast quickened me, and I sucked in heavy drafts of ocean breeze, like a person who has just fled a burning building.

Along the shoreline swirls of black sand sparkled like veins of tiny sequins. It didn't have to be this beautiful. God could have made sand dull, like dirt, like so many rocks. He didn't have to make colors, or eyes capable of discerning them. But He did. What other wondrous works hath God wrought which my eyes have never seen? What fresh marvels await, I wondered, when the world is made new?

On the drive back, I stopped at Vons for a snack, a peach with an artistic produce sticker. Peeling it off, I remembered that years ago, when the children were small, I used to collect fruit stickers. When Mom discovered this, she began setting aside the prettier ones, affixing them onto a note card, and periodically sending them to me in an envelope with coupons for things she thought I might buy, along with comics she had clipped from newspapers. I hadn't received any envelopes like this for a long time. I suddenly wished I could thank Mom for thinking of me all the time. For trying to make my life better. For sending a fat little packet of love every couple of months, something that said, "I know what you like, what you buy, what makes you laugh, and I want to share these with you."

In the parking lot, I folded my forearms over the top of the steering wheel, lowered my head, and sobbed. Loudly, in the way you can only do in an empty house or in a car with the windows up. I muttered, in an appalling, choking voice, "I'm sorry, Mom. I'm sorry."

And I knew, somehow, she'd already forgiven me. She always loved me. She was always saying it, with words and strawberries and clean laundry and envelopes in the mail. Mom wasn't perfect, but she loved me. She couldn't give me everything I wanted, but she gave me what she had. Her love outlived her senses, and it still hovered in the atmosphere, like the sea air. I'd been breathing it in all this time, hadn't I?

She gave me what she had, and I tolerated her. She shared her life with me, and I judged her. But she forgave me in advance. Mom threw all my offenses overboard years ago. She had forgotten every wrong. God remembered, but He had forgiven. Already He was peeling the guilt away, as I sat in the car, calling my sins by name between sobs. Somewhere outside of time, Jesus collected up my transgressions in a bottle, clapped the lid on it, and threw it into the ocean.

Later, when I pulled into our driveway, my feet were breaded with glittery black sand and my eyes were clear. I felt as if I'd been scrubbed clean.

STEADY AS SHE GOES

JULY 2015

*W*hen I got back from New Jersey, Mom looked worse than ever. She slept and slept, unresponsive to touch, to voices, to everything. It was almost impossible to get her to eat or drink. We crushed up the pills and mixed them with water, then dribbled this slurry under her tongue, to be absorbed directly into her bloodstream.

With Rachel's blessing, we took her off some medications. I wrote to Michael, who would visit soon, that she might die while he was here.

When Claire gently moved Mom's hand, she cried out. Why was there more pain? Was it just in her arm, or all over? She murmured, "I'm so *sore.*"

Linda brought eucalyptus oil and rubbed it carefully on Mom's knees, elbows and wrists. I forgot to send her the memo about massage oils. Oh, well. It was too late now.

Then, amazingly, Mom went back to ...normal? I checked on her one afternoon, and she said, "Susan, I love you to pieces."

She hadn't called me by name in weeks, or said a coherent sentence, either.

I showed her a photo of baby Marshall, and she said, "Isn't he just the sweetest little thing?" She was as lucid as ever.

Maybe the sight of Marshall made her decide she'd like to live a while longer. She had always loved babies. Or maybe the it was eucalyptus oil. Who can tell?

LINDA WAS one of the most life-giving people I knew. When she arrived in the morning, she greeted my mother cheerily by name and set about making things fresh and clean and comfortable. She opened the window, changed Mom's briefs, turned her, fluffed the pillows, smoothed the blankets. She was mindful of Mom's skin, and took care to see that she didn't stay in one position too long.

When Ginny complained of pain in her legs, Linda rubbed them with arnica cream. One day I found her gently manipulating my mother's right leg, stretching, bending and massaging. She was playing a CD of relaxing piano music, and an exotic smell hung in the air.

"Mmmmm! What's that?" I asked.

"It's a blend of bergamot and lavender essential oils. It's supposed to help people relax."

"It smells lovely."

"I know, right?" she smiled tranquilly, as she slowly bent Mom's ankle and rotated it. Linda was the kind of person who brought her lunch of a spinach smoothie and power salad in a floral-print hemp bag.

"You really go above and beyond," I went on. "I really appreciate the fact that you go to every length to make my mother comfortable."

"Aw," she beamed, smoothing scented lotion onto Mom's wasted calf. "She's such a sweetie."

Mom interrupted imperiously: "Don't you be throwing me back and forth like a dog, would you please?"

Another complete sentence. Linda and I looked at each other and grinned.

ACTIVELY DYING

NOVEMBER 2015

*M*om was so skinny now that it was very hard to keep her bones from poking through her skin. We redoubled our efforts at repositioning frequently, but red spots kept appearing on her shoulders, hips or pelvic bones. We already had padded foot cradles to protect the skin on Mom's heels. Now Claire ordered a sheepskin to protect her shoulder blades, and Linda set to work fashioning a foam cradle for Mom's right ear and another for her hip bone. What we really needed was breathable bubble wrap.

Increasingly, Cassidy and Linda were reporting that Mom was "in a lot of pain." Claire and I noticed it too. Mom cried out when turned, though we moved slowly and gently. Today, she just kept groaning. When we offered water, she didn't respond. We put the straw between her lips, but she just looked at us. She finally swallowed in one laborious push.

Claire made breakfast, but her heart wasn't in it. Mom couldn't eat. She just fell asleep.

Mom didn't sleep like a normal person any more. She grimaced, curling her upper lip and baring her teeth, jaw hanging slack. Her face was so gaunt it looked like a skull mask. The skin over her forehead and cheekbones was stretched smooth, making her look freakishly younger. I had read about dying people having "sunken eyes." I always wondered what that meant. Now I knew. The flesh had melted all around her eye sockets, leaving a large hollow of unwrinkled skin and making her eyes appear larger. In this new aspect, Mom resembled Munch's *The Scream*.

But I was glad she slept. When Mom slept, I could imagine she wasn't feeling any pain. Maybe she was dreaming of Granny, or of picking her beloved Texas bluebonnets beneath stacks of plumy clouds.

Rachel was visiting more often now. She sketched the end-of-life scenario, warning us about the death rattle. We thanked her politely, knowing Mom would pull out of this one too.

Ginny now needed morphine every two hours. I began staying up till midnight to give her a sublingual morphine slurry. Claire, Arthur and I cobbled together a schedule and took turns. This way, we could all get at least six hours of uninterrupted sleep. When Arthur came in at 2:00am, and Claire at 4:00am, I didn't hear them at all. My alarm went off at 6:00am, and I was ready to do it all again.

How long can a person live without water? I'd always

read that it was two weeks. It sounded like a very uncomfortable two weeks to me. But I'd wager the morphine helped a lot.

A few days later, Rachel sat at the dining room table and asked how we were doing. When we told her about our morphine schedule, she pulled out her cell phone and started making calls. "It's time to call in crisis care," she said. "Let's let daughters be daughters."

Rachel told us that Mom was "actively dying," but I still didn't believe her.

The people hospice sent over for crisis care were quiet, unobtrusive, and efficient. Each one brought a mysterious little satchel and swiftly set up shop in Mom's room. When I entered this morning, I was greeted by Sacha, who was just finishing up her shift. Soon she would pack up her equipment and quietly withdraw, and someone else would knock on our door and trundle a little rolling bag over the stone tiles to Mom's room.

Mom looked the same, her skin like parchment across her cachectic cheekbones. She wasn't grimacing now. No more Munch. Her breaths were deep and infrequent. Deborah sometimes stole into Mom's room and stood by the bed quietly holding her hand. Deborah knew.

What would it be like, I wondered, when they took her away? Somehow, it was very important that Mom should wear clothes when her body was taken away. And that hateful catheter removed, finally. I wanted her mouth to be closed and her hair to be combed. She should not look unkempt.

Two years ago, when we thought she could attend

Jesse's wedding, I bought Mom a deep blue shirt and eggplant-colored pants. Today I pulled these out of her closet and held them up for Claire. "Do you think these will be okay to put on her?" I asked. I didn't add, "when she dies."

Claire looked stricken, but nodded her okay. If it turned out to be another bump in the road, we could put that outfit right back into the closet. It would keep.

For days after Mom stopped drinking, the catheter bag still collected urine. Her kidneys were plugging away. When I walked into Mom's room this morning, the bag was empty. I asked the caregiver, "Did you empty it already?"

"No, she hasn't produced any urine all the time I've been here."

So this was it, then.

What was the last thing I said to her, when she was awake? I didn't remember. But neither did she, so maybe it didn't matter. Did she feel my love now, feeble as I was at showing it and as far gone as she was? I leaned in close and whispered, "I love you, Mom. We're still here for you. We love you."

I pressed my ear to her chest, and heard a strong beat.

How long can a person live without water? We would see.

RELEASED

*E*ntering Mom's room two days later, I was pleased
at how neat she looked. The caregiver had
washed her face and smoothed the blankets. Mom's
breathing was more labored. Her heartbeat, fainter. I put
my lips to her ear and said, "I love you, Mom. We're here
for you." I straightened up a minute, then leaned over and
whispered, "It's okay for you to go now. We'll be okay. We
have each other, and we have Jesus. You go on ahead of us,
and we'll see you when we get there."

~

CLAIRE, Arthur, Deb and I were just hanging around the
house. We didn't want to go anyplace, and couldn't pull
ourselves together enough to do anything productive. We
were simply waiting. Arthur was sitting with Mom, so
Claire said, "Let's play Take Two."

We spread out the letter tiles on the table for our word game. It would take our mind off Mom for a while. We had just finished a round when Arthur walked in and said, "She's gone."

We stared up at him, uncomprehending. He added, "She just stopped breathing. I was there when she took her last breath."

Claire and Deb and I hastened to Mom's bedside to see for ourselves. She lay slightly to one side, as usual, and appeared to be sleeping. Her skin was smoother than ever, waxlike over her forehead and cheekbones. But the room was strangely tranquil. I'd grown used to her ragged, laborious breathing, and its absence created a sacred stillness.

Some people say that a person's presence hovers about the room after they die. Maybe Mom's spirit was there that day, hanging back to catch a last glimpse of her daughters. If it was, she would have seen Arthur holding Claire as she stood weeping. She would have seen me collapsing onto my own mattress in unguarded tears, and Deborah kneeling down to pull me into her arms. She would have known her work here was done.

THE CALIFORNIA MEMORIAL

JANUARY 2016

*C*laire and I wept that day as if our mother's death had been unexpected. Mom gave us plenty of notice, though. So I had no excuse, sitting here in this room full of mourners, to feel unprepared. But who wants to plan a funeral, ever?

Before Mom got sick, when I thought of her death, it was in a fuzzy and theoretical future. I never thought of the actual process of dying. I skipped ahead to the pretty parts, like you see in the movies. Somebody, not me, would arrange a funeral in a Baptist church in Ballinger. There would be elderly Baptists in attendance, weeping with quiet restraint, or, more likely, sitting in the pews like stony statues, hands folded. After the pastor's brief but intensely evangelistic devotional, my sister and I, the aunts and cousins and friends, would pile into cars and proceed along red dirt roads, past pecan trees and fields of sorghum, kicking up clouds of dust, to a cemetery. Under the glaring expanse of sky, a gleaming mahogany casket would be lowered into the ground. Someone would attempt, unsuccessfully, to suppress a loud sob. The pastor would offer a prayer, and Claire would throw in the first dense clod of Texas earth. And then we'd eat. There would be fried chicken and cornbread and beans and watermelon and pecan pie and sweet tea dense enough to make us cough. Even though Claire and I would be all broken up, our relatives would urge us to eat. And tearfully, we'd manage to do so.

We weren't getting the decorous Texas funeral. Instead, I was in the living room of the Amazingly Large House. Assembled around me on sofas and chairs and loveseats were a handful of Mom's California relatives and the faithful Linda. And there was no glossy casket. Mom chose cremation. Two months ago the people from the Neptune Society came and took her body away in a van. I didn't watch them do it. The Neptune Society was taking its sweet time, so there wasn't even an urn with ashes on which we could awkwardly focus our morbid attention.

And there was no pastor. Instead, we were listening to Claire read a carefully-crafted eulogy. She shared some happy memories: how Mom encouraged us to go outside and get dirty making mud pies, how she sewed glamorous outfits for our Barbie dolls, how she spent hours chemically straightening Claire's frizzy hair.

That time she took us to a cabin at Big Bear Lake, way outside her comfort zone, where we went on a hike and encountered, to our great surprise, a real live bear.

Claire described how my mother devoted many hours to helping Granny straighten out her bank accounts. I remembered now that the dining room table shuddered every time she made an entry on the hulking metal adding machine, while I sprawled belly-down on the shag rug below, crafting an intricate cardboard house for my Barbie doll, oblivious. Back then, I never paid attention to what my mother was doing unless it affected me directly.

Next to me on the squishy leather couch were Jesse and Dinae with little Jack, who noisily extracted toy cars from a Ziploc bag. Deborah was perched on the edge of a chair with unwavering attention, and Arthur sat quietly with hands folded. Cousin Rosemary was there, with her daughter Maureen. There was not one elderly Baptist in attendance that day.

Claire's voice caught as she remembered how Mom used to take us to church and answer our questions about God as best she could. "This training," my sister explained, "provided the foundation for our spiritual formation as followers of Jesus. If I could thank my Mom for one thing, this would definitely be it."

One by one, we shared memories: Ginny playing word games, cutting coupons, taking meals to shut-ins, playing games on the floor with her young grandchildren. Linda called Mom "sweet." I had not thought of my mother as "sweet." And yet that word came up again and again. Sweet, kind, fun. She was certainly fun, in her day. She had a great sense of humor, when she still had senses.

Deborah read a passage of scripture and Arthur spoke

briefly; Jesse offered a prayer, and Joel led us in singing "Give Me Jesus."

Then we relaxed and ate. Some clustered around photos of Ginny. My favorite was one Dad took shortly after their marriage. She stands on the grass in a full-skirted cotton dress, ramrod-straight, hands behind her back. She's smiling tolerantly as if he has just said something slightly exasperating. The photo is black and white, but I've colorized it in my mind: her eyes are a brilliant blue, the dress is navy, and her lipstick is cherry-colored. Carefully-arranged chestnut waves frame her wide forehead and curl around shining button-shaped earrings. She's crafting a playful retort to lob at my father when the photo session is over.

As Maureen took her leave, she shyly apologized, "I hardly knew your mother, so I didn't have any memories to share."

"But you listened to our stories," I told her. "And that was what we needed."

PICKING UP THE ASHES

The website read, "The offices of the Neptune Society are located across from AutoZone and Immigration Services." Thirteen years ago, in this same office, an urn containing my father's ashes was placed in Claire's hands. She was surprised by a wave of grief, and found herself weeping alone on a brown Naugahyde chair in the foyer. So this time she brought me for moral support.

The Neptune lady crisply located Mom's file and guided us to a small table. We signed the paperwork and walked away bearing a handsome mahogany urn in a paper shopping bag, "like a Victoria's Secret bag," muttered Claire, disapprovingly. She was always a little cranky when her heart was hurting. This time, there were no tears. Perhaps I'd been a bulwark of strength. Or maybe we'd both cried enough already.

SECURITY

I booked a flight to Texas. When Claire joined me the following week, we'd drive out to meet Mom's relatives in San Saba for a second memorial.

So I here I was going through security again. Bagged toiletries, no water, no metal, no Swiss Army knife. I got this. The TSA agent squinted at the screen. "Do you have something metal in there?" he asked, pointing to my blue carry-on.

Time to focus. "Oh, right. That must be the urn. That's my mom's ashes. I'm going to a memorial."

"Can you bring the bag over there?" he said, indicating one of those stainless steel tables. "Will you open it so I can have a look?" He kept his eyes on me and spoke carefully, as if negotiating the release of a hostage.

I hoisted the bag up and unzipped it, revealing the urn.

He pulled some gloves and a wand from somewhere and asked, "May I open it?"

Something big and hairy inside me rose up and growled *NO*. Outwardly, I shrugged and said flatly, "Do what you have to do." I stood with arms crossed as he oh-so-gingerly ran the wand over the outside of the box, then opened it and undid the plastic bag.

I felt the hair on my scalp standing up as it did when I became angry. I thought, *Don't you dare touch my mother*. Which was completely irrational.

The agent closed up everything, turned to me and said, "You're supposed to let us know in advance you're bringing ashes through security."

Thanks, I thought. *I'll remember that next time my mother dies*. I repacked my bag, fuming silently, and trundled off to get some tea to calm my nerves. Tea has a civilizing influence. I needed some civilizing about now.

DEMENTIA ISN'T FOR EVERYONE

MAY 2016
LAKE BELTON, TEXAS

I couldn't stay at Mom's Temple house anymore, so I turned once again to Zoe, who put me in contact with a hospitable church friend. Maxine served as a missionary in Tanzania along with Michael and Dorris, who had impressed me with their ten- to fifteen-year plan for Neema House, an infant rescue center.

I had a few days to relax at Maxine's before Claire arrived, so I spent the time scouting out food for the memorial and getting to know my hostess. Maxine took care of her husband for a number of years in their home, after he developed Parkinson's Disease. As we sat on her back porch watching the sun set over Lake Belton, she described the hands-on care she rendered and the mistakes she made. But Maxine didn't spend much energy looking back. Mostly, she lived in the present, participating in church ministries, dogsitting, keeping in touch with far-flung family members, and making guests like me feel completely at home.

While at Maxine's, I lunched with Zoe. The hip food scene had made its way up the 35 to Temple. Megg's Cafe offered diners "modern and innovative Central Texas cuisine" and promised a "fun, relaxed, simple yet layered dining experience." I was down for that.

As we awaited our hand-crafted pork-belly banh mi and deviled farm eggs with warm bacon marmalade, I updated Zoe on Ginny's story, and she, in turn, shared her story. She and her husband constantly visited, monitored and helped their parents, three of whom had dementia. Falls, joint-replacement surgeries, medications, weight loss and confusion were taking their toll. It could just be me, but I was seeing dementia everywhere.

But then there was Maxine, in her late seventies, who approached life like a sumo wrestler. Her mind was sharp, and she had energy to spare. She took photos of sunsets, and her pets and church family, and posted them on Facebook. She kept up with the babies at Neema House and prayed for them. While I was there, she hosted a cousin she hadn't seen in decades.

And there were Michael and Dorris, in their seventies, working hard in Africa, and loving it.

There was Aunt Bobbie, still sharp and strong, enjoying life.

No, not everyone got dementia. Not everyone got frail and frightened as they aged.

There were no restaurants in San Saba that appealed to me, so I placed an order at Megg's. But Megg's didn't offer pecan pie. When I told Maxine the sad news, she shot back, "I have five pounds of pecans in my freezer. I'll make you a pie."

"No, no," I insisted. "That's too much."

She waved away my objection. "It's no trouble at all," she said, yanking open the freezer. "Besides, I make very good pies."

THE SAN SABA MEMORIAL

*C*laire and I picked up the food at Megg's and drove to the Methodist church in San Saba. Soon Bobbie and one of her daughters joined us, and some cousins arrived. Lou was too ill to attend, and we couldn't even locate John.

In the fellowship hall, I set out the photos of Ginny, and we took seats around the long folding tables with wood-like veneer. Once again, Claire and I shared our memories and invited others to share theirs. Then we pulled out the boxes of food from Megg's and began to tuck in. Maxine's pie was a hit. Once again, my mother's memorial service was not what I thought it would be. Whatever made me think I could plan anything?

We packed the leftovers, put the chairs back and wiped the tables. Then somebody had the idea to go out to the cemetery. So off we went.

I'd never been to the cemetery in San Saba, but it was

eerily like the one I imagined. We twisted and wound our way through back roads and cool oak groves. The road dipped to traverse a shallow stream over a little splintery bridge. Up the hill again and through the cemetery gate. Our tires kicked up clouds of red dust. We followed our cousin's truck and pulled over onto the grass near the family plot, piling out of our cars and fanning out amongst the headstones under the blinding blue sky, the wind whipping hair into our eyes. And that was how I saw my grandmother's grave marker for the first time. Bobbie pointed it out for Claire and me. I knelt and brushed off some dead grass clippings. Funny, I had never thought to ask where Granny was buried. I felt she was still alive somewhere. She, and the pink and white house in Waco with its peach trees and tomato plants, floated perpetually on the perimeter of my imagination. I would see her again. If my understanding of the Bible is correct, Mom was now with her beloved Mama. Maybe they were eating pecan pie.

ONE LAST THING

omorrow Claire and I would fly back to California. But there was one thing left to do.

We pulled into a deserted parking lot across the street from a field of vivid red and yellow blossoms. I opened my Bible to Genesis 3:19 and read:

> *By the sweat of your face*
> *You will eat bread,*
> *Till you return to the ground,*
> *Because from it you were taken;*
> *For you are dust,*
> *And to dust you shall return.*

The LORD God had formed man of dust from the ground, and breathed into his nostrils the breath of life. But the man and the woman severed their connection with

God for a bite of fruit, and could not be trusted near the tree of life in their compromised condition, lest they should "take also from the tree of life, and eat, and live forever." Ashes to ashes, dust to dust.

But Jesus came to undo that, so I must read further.

The Apostle Paul writes in 1 Corinthians 15.

> *The body, sown like a seed, dies, but is raised to new life. It is sown in dishonor, it is raised in glory; it is sown in weakness, it is raised in power; it is sown a natural body, it is raised a spiritual body.*

For the hundredth time I wondered, *What's a spiritual body?* I believed it, but I didn't get it. It had to be a different kind of physical body than the one we had currently. So much better. Permanent, glorious, new.

Flesh and blood cannot inherit the kingdom of God. The perishable cannot inherit the imperishable.

> *So when this corruptible shall have put on incorruption, and this mortal shall have put on immortality, then shall be brought to pass the saying that is written,*
> *Death is swallowed up in victory.*
> *O death, where is thy sting?*
> *O grave, where is thy victory?*
> *The sting of death is sin; and the strength of sin is the law. But thanks be to God, which giveth us the victory through our Lord Jesus Christ.*

Claire gently took my hand, and we prayed. We thanked God for his goodness to us and to our mom, and one last time we entrusted her soul and body to his care.

We pulled the double-bagged ashes from the urn. I hefted the thick plastic bag, estimating its weight at about three pounds. This was all that was left of Mom's body, the body that bore and nurtured us, the body that rocked me and bathed me and bandaged my skinned knees. The body I loved and hated, turned and fed and finally wept over.

Claire and I ran across the road and picked our way through a field of Indian Blankets, Indian Paintbrush, and mimosa. The meadow was fairly shouting with red, yellow and orange flowers.

"Look," exclaimed Claire. "Bluebonnets!" She stooped to pick a few. Their season was past, but next spring they'd come up again, covering the field in riotous indigo. We liked the idea of Mom being in the bluebonnets. Together we shook the bag's whitish-gray contents out over the mass of fiery blossoms, making sure the wind was blowing away from us.

AFTERWORD

Vista, California

One Sunday after the worship service, Pastor Dan invited anyone to come forward for prayer. I elbowed my way down and approached a thin lady in a metallic gold blouse, with hair bleached blonde. *Barbie again*, I thought. But I'd wised up by now.

I told Barbie I'd recently inherited assets and really, really wanted to use my inheritance for the Kingdom of God. She clasped my hands in her manicured fingers and began to pray, "Lord, Susan needs Your wisdom. She needs to know how to use everything you've given her for Your kingdom. Not only her financial assets, but her whole inheritance. She has stories to tell, Lord. She has a history to share with others. This is part of her inheritance, Lord, how You've worked in her life. Help her to use all she has for You." I felt my face distorting in that awful way it does when I'm trying not to cry. I hadn't said anything about writing a book. Tears began oozing from my eyes, and I was afraid snot would start dripping out of my nose too.

When we finished, I ran my nose across my sleeve and told her about the book. "Oh," she smiled. "I've published three books and I'm working on a fourth. Once when I was getting on a plane for the umpteenth time on a book tour, I told God, 'I'm too old for this,' and He said to me, 'No, now you're old enough to do this.'"

Barbie, whose real name turned out to be Marilee,

mused, "I almost didn't come to church today because I just got back from a trip and I'm leaving for another trip tomorrow. But now I know why I came today." She hugged me. "When I get back in about a month, let's go out for coffee."

I pulled myself together and headed for the exit, eager to have a supplementary cry in the car. It was easier, now, to shed tears, but also easier to stop when I was finished. But by the time I got there, I didn't feel like crying any more. For now, I guessed, I was all done with crying.

ACKNOWLEDGMENTS

Deciding to write a book is a little bit like deciding to have a baby. It's pretty exciting to start, but takes considerable grit to see the whole thing through. And, similarly, you need a lot of help.

Thanks to my daughter Deborah, who scrawled "boring" in red pen over half my manuscript in its infancy, sparing later readers; to my uncle Jerry, who did what he could; to my Aunt Bobbie, who filled in some memory gaps; to my kind and tactful editor Cindy Rinaman Marsch, who continued Deborah's ministrations with greater specificity; to generous, gentle and helpful beta readers Katrina Kirkwood, Boni Wagner-Stafford, Dixie Marie Carlton, Maria Masters, Julie Ris and Jo Ullah; to my sister, who lived it with me and then had to read about it, and her husband, who encouraged me at every opportunity with unflagging optimism; to my children, Benjamin, Rebekah, Deborah and Michael, for their love and support;

to Christian brothers and sisters everywhere who loved me without reason and without question; and to God, who has graciously included me in the story.

96972724R00189

Made in the USA
Middletown, DE
03 November 2018